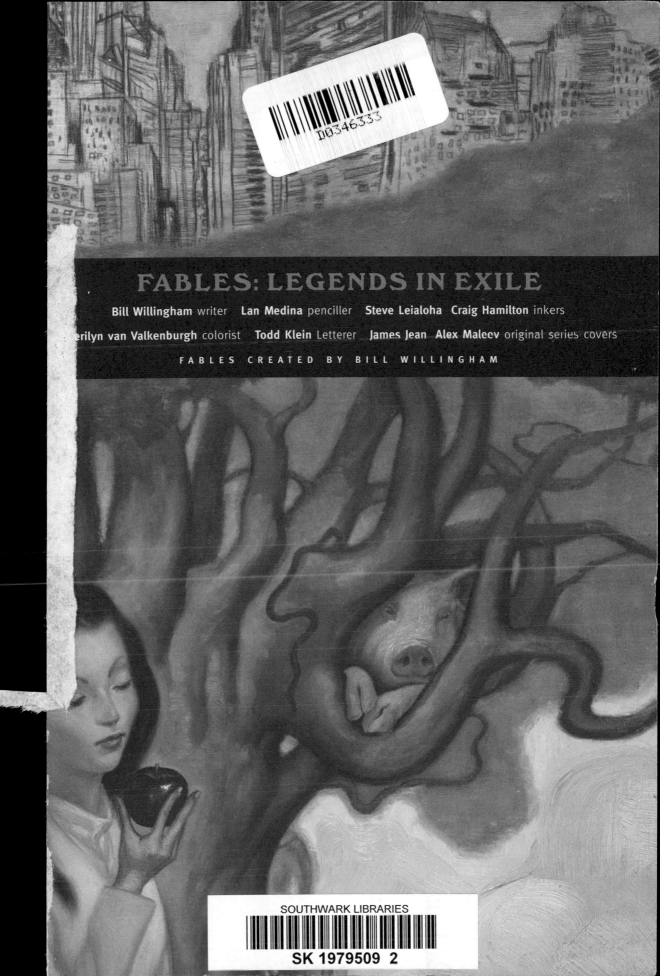

FABLES: LEGENDS IN EXILE

Bill Willingham writer **Lan Medina** penciller **Steve Leialoha** **Craig Hamilton** inkers

erilyn van Valkenburgh colorist **Todd Klein** Letterer **James Jean** **Alex Maleev** original series covers

FABLES CREATED BY BILL WILLINGHAM

KAREN BERGER VP-Executive Editor **SHELLY BOND** Senior Editor-original series **SCOTT NYBAKKEN** Editor-collected edition
ROBBIN BROSTERMAN Senior Art Director **PAUL LEVITZ** President & Publisher
GEORG BREWER VP-Design & Retail Product Development **RICHARD BRUNING** Senior VP-Creative Director
PATRICK CALDON Senior VP-Finance & Operations **CHRIS CARAMALIS** VP-Finance **TERRI CUNNINGHAM** VP-Managing Editor
STEPHANIE FIERMAN Senior VP-Sales & Marketing **ALISON GILL** VP-Manufacturing **RICH JOHNSON** VP-Book Trade Sales
HANK KANALZ VP-General Manager, WildStorm **LILLIAN LASERSON** Senior VP & General Counsel
JIM LEE Editorial Director-WildStorm **PAULA LOWITT** Senior VP-Business & Legal Affairs
DAVID MCKILLIPS VP-Advertising & Custom Publishing **JOHN NEE** VP-Business Development
GREGORY NOVECK Senior VP-Creative Affairs **CHERYL RUBIN** Senior VP-Brand Management **BOB WAYNE** VP-Sales

F A B L E S :   L E G E N D S   I N   E X I L E

DC Comics, 1700 Broadway, New York, NY 10019
A Warner Bros. Entertainment Company
Printed in USA. 9/1/2010. Ninth Printing.
ISBN: 978-1-56389-942-3.
Cover illustration by James Jean.

To Shelly Bond
Intrepid Vertigo editor, who insisted on taking FABLES when I was trying to sell her another idea entirely.
— Bill Willingham

ONCE UPON A TIME...

HURRY!

IN A FICTIONAL LAND CALLED NEW YORK CITY.

CAN'T YOU GO FASTER?

CAN'T YOU PLEASE TO BE HOLDING ONTO YOUR WATER, SIR? YOU ARE VERY MUCH TO BE MAKING ME A NERVOUS DRIVER.

KEEP THE CHANGE.

AND WHAT CHANGE WOULD THAT BE, SIR? YOU ARE TO BE GIVING ME, ACCORDING TO THE METER, TWENTY-FIVE CENTS MORE!

CHAPTER ONE:
OLD TALES REVISITED

In which we meet many of our principal players and get just the first hint or two of some of the myriad troubles to come.

Written by **Bill Willingham** Pencilled by **Lan Medina** Inked by **Steve Leialoha**

Lettered by **Todd Klein** Colored by Sherilyn **van Valkenburgh** Separated by **Zylenol**

Cover art by **James Jean & Alex Maleev** Assistant Editor **Mariah Huehner** Editor **Shelly Bond**

FABLES is created by Bill Willingham

BULLFINCH STREET

KIPLING STREET

BIGBY!

SECURITY
OFFICE

B. WOLF

YOU LOOK OUT OF BREATH, JACK. BEEN CLIMBING *BEANSTALKS* AGAIN?

huh...huh... NO.

BLOWN DOWN ANY PIGGIES' *HOMES* LATELY?

I'M A BIT *BUSY*, JACK. DID YOU RUN ALL THE WAY OVER HERE JUST TO TRADE *VERBAL BARBS*, OR IS THERE SOMETHING ELSE YOU NEED?

THERE WAS -- THERE IS -- A TERRIBLE THING -- A CRIME --

A *TERRIBLE THING* HAPPENED!

AS *SORRY* AS I AM FOR YOUR MARITAL "*DIFFICULTIES*," IT ISN'T ANY OF MY BUSINESS. WE *BARELY* HAVE ENOUGH MONEY AND MANPOWER TO RUN THE MOST *BASIC* OF UNDER-GROUND GOVERNMENT SERVICES.

WE CAN'T *AFFORD* TO DO MARITAL COUNSELING, AND TO BE PERFECTLY *CANDID*, I WOULDN'T ALLOW IT IF WE *COULD*.

THE *MUNDANES* MAY LOOK TO THEIR GOVERNMENT TO SOLVE THEIR PROBLEMS, BUT IN THE *FABLE* COMMUNITY, WE *EXPECT* YOU TO BE ABLE TO RUN YOUR *OWN* LIVES.

OUR *ONLY* CONCERN IS THAT YOU'RE CURRENTLY IN VIOLATION OF OUR MOST *VITAL* LAW: NO FABLE SHALL, BY: ACTION OR INACTION, CAUSE OUR MAGICAL NATURE TO BECOME KNOWN TO THE MUNDANE WORLD.

SNOW WHITE
DIRECTOR OF OPERATIONS

IF YOU CAN'T *MAINTAIN* A NORMAL *HUMAN* APPEAR-ANCE OR PURCHASE A CON-CEALING *GLAMOUR* FROM ONE OF OUR *WITCHES*--

--OUR RULES MANDATE THAT YOU BE *RELOCATED* UPSTATE TO THE *FARM*, WHERE ALL THE OTHER NONHUMAN FABLES LIVE.

BUT WE DIDN'T *ESCAPE* FROM THE HOMELANDS WITH OUR FORTUNE *INTACT!* WE CAN'T *AFFORD* A GLAMOUR POWERFUL ENOUGH TO HIDE MY HUSBAND'S CURSE. WE *BARELY* MAKE ENOUGH BETWEEN US TO GET *BY*.

UND ITH THOTH THAME MONEY TWUBBLES THAT EXATHERBATHES OWAH MAWITAL PWOBWEMS AND MAKTH THE CURTH COME BACK.

AS *SYMPATHETIC* AS I AM TO YOUR TROUBLES, I CAN'T BE OF ANY *HELP* TO YOU.

MANY OF THE FABLES--I'D EVEN SAY *MOST* OF US--LOST OUR LANDS, TITLES AND FORTUNES WHEN WE WERE FORCED *OUT* OF OUR HOMELANDS BY THE *ADVERSARY*.

WE HAVE TO MAKE DO AS *BEST* WE CAN.

SNOW WHITE
DIRECTOR OF OPERATIONS

TRUE, I'M NOT REALLY THE MAYOR OF FABLETOWN, ONLY HIS DEPUTY. AND IF YOU WANT TO MAKE AN APPOINTMENT TO TELL YOUR TALE OF WOE *DIRECTLY* TO KING COLE, THAT'S *YOUR* PREROGATIVE.

BUT I'LL TELL YOU RIGHT NOW WHAT WILL HAPPEN. HE'LL LISTEN TO YOU AND MAKE ALL THE RIGHT NOISES ABOUT HOW *SORRY* HE IS FOR YOUR PLIGHT--AND HIS SYMPATHY WILL BE GENUINE BECAUSE HE'S A WONDERFUL, *EMPATHETIC* MAN.

AND THEN THE MOMENT YOU'RE OUT THE DOOR, HE'LL ASK *ME* WHAT *I* WANT TO DO ABOUT IT, BECAUSE THAT'S HOW WE WORK. HE DOES ALL THE FORMAL *GLADHANDING*. HE MAKES THE OFFICIAL APPEARANCES AND HOSTS THE CEREMONIAL FUNCTIONS. AND I DO THE *REAL* WORK OF RUNNING OUR COMMUNITY.

FOR BETTER OR **WORSE**, YOU'VE JUST HAD YOUR **APPEAL** TO CITY HALL.

YOU DIVORCED **YOUR** PRINCE **CENTURIES** AGO. YOU HAVE **NO IDEA** HOW HARD IT IS TO KEEP A MARRIAGE GOING SO LONG.

NOWAH, DEAH. THEWES NO WEASON TO GET **PERSONOAH.**

SNOW WHITE
DIRECTOR OF ...RATIONS

DON'T GET **PERSONAL?** AFTER SHE OPENLY **CRITICIZED** OUR MARRIED LIFE?

I DID **NO SUCH** THING.

AND JUST WHO IS **SHE** TO CRITICIZE **ANYONE'S** PERSONAL LIFE, AFTER WHAT **I** HEARD ABOUT HER TAWDRY LITTLE ADVENTURE WITH THOSE SEVEN DWARVES?

OKAY, FOLKS, BUSINESS IS PILING **UP** AND WE NEED TO MOVE THINGS ALONG TO MISS WHITE'S **NEXT** APPOINTMENT.

SNOW WHITE
~~~~~

BUT--?

12

THANK YOU *BOTH* FOR COMING IN. OUR DOOR IS *ALWAYS* OPEN.

BUT WE WEREN'T *FINISHED!*

YES YOU WERE, MA'AM, ASSUMING YOU HOPED TO *SURVIVE* YOUR LAST COMMENT. TAKE MY ADVICE, SOME TOPICS ARE BEST NEVER BROUGHT UP.

NEVER DISCUSS PERSONAL HYGIENE WITH A BRIDGE TROLL. *NEVER* TRADE CASSEROLE RECIPES WITH A BLACK FOREST WITCH. BUT *ABOVE ALL*, WHEN TALKING TO THE DEPUTY MAYOR--

--NEVER MENTION THE DWARVES!

SECURITY OFFICE
B. WOLF

GOODBYE, MISS BEAUTY. MISTER BEAST. TAKE *CARE*, NOW.

BLUE BOY--

IS HER ROYAL *NIBS* IN?

YES, BUT SHE'S IN A *FOUL* MOOD.

I'M ABOUT TO MAKE IT *WORSE.*

ARE YOU ENJOYING YOUR *LUNCH,* SIR?

VERY MUCH SO. THANK YOU, *MOLLY.*

AND HOW DID YOU FIND YOUR *STEAK?*

I SIMPLY LOOKED BEHIND THE *POTATO* AND THERE IT *WAS.*

Gottfried's STEAK HOUSE

OH MY, THAT'S VERY *CLEVER.* YOU'RE A *DELIGHTFULLY* CLEVER MAN. POSITIVELY...

CLEVER?

UHM...YES. SO, WILL THERE BE ANYTHING ELSE, SIR?

NOTHING MORE TO EAT OR DRINK, MISS, BUT WE'VE SHARED SUCH A NICE *FLIRTATION* THIS AFTERNOON THAT I'M *TEMPTED* TO ASK YOU FOR YOUR PHONE NUMBER.

I'M TEMPTED TO GIVE IT.

ACTUALLY, I'M ABOUT TO GO *OFF SHIFT* AND I'M TEMPTED TO ASK YOU TO COME HOME WITH ME RIGHT *NOW.*

THAT'S A DELIGHTFUL IDEA, DEAR MISS MOLLY, BUT I'M AFRAID THAT WOULD CREATE A SLIGHT PROBLEM FOR ONE OR *BOTH* OF US.

I CAME IN HERE WITH-OUT A PENNY TO MY NAME, AND MY *PLAN* WAS TO EAT A FILLING MEAL AND THEN SKIP OUT ON THE CHECK.

BUT IF I'M TO GO HOME *WITH* YOU -- WELL, WE'RE SUDDENLY FACED WITH A RATHER *AWKWARD* MOMENT.

REALLY? YOU'RE *BROKE?*

COMPLETELY AND UTTERLY.

BUT YOU'D *LIKE* TO COME BACK WITH ME TO MY PLACE?

THAT IS CURRENTLY MY *FONDEST* DESIRE.

WELL, I *GUESS* I CAN AFFORD TO PICK UP THE CHECK SINCE I WOULD HAVE BEEN STUCK WITH IT *ANYWAY*, IF YOU'D SNUCK OUT.

YOU'RE A GOOD SPORT, MOLLY. I *ADORE* YOU ALREADY.

SINCE WE'RE JUST *MINUTES* AWAY FROM DOING WONDERFULLY NASTY THINGS TO EACH OTHER, DON'T YOU THINK IT'S TIME I LEARNED YOUR NAME?

I'M PRINCE CHARMING, OF COURSE.

THAT'S FOR SURE.

BUT SERIOUSLY, WHO *ARE* YOU?

I'M EMBARRASSED TO *ADMIT* THAT I'D ACTUALLY HAVE TO FETCH MY WALLET TO RECALL *WHICH* IDENTITY I'M USING THESE DAYS.

IS IT *REALLY* SO IMPORTANT, DARLING?

WHAT DO YOU *NEED*, MISTER WOLF? I'M *BUSY* RIGHT NOW.

YOU NEED TO PREPARE YOURSELF FOR SOME *BAD* NEWS, SNOW.

DON'T BE SO *DRAMATIC.* I ALREADY KNOW. MY *EX* IS BACK IN TOWN.

THANK YOU FOR NOT SMOKING

SNOW WHITE DIRECTOR OF OPERATIONS

APPARENTLY, HE MANAGED TO FINALLY WEAR OUT HIS WELCOME AMONG EVEN THE MOST *INBRED* ELEMENTS OF EUROPEAN ROYALTY.

THIS *ISN'T* ABOUT PRINCE CHARMING. IT'S ABOUT YOUR *SISTER,* ROSE RED.

THIS MAY *SURPRISE* YOU, MISTER WOLF, BUT I'M NOT *ENTIRELY* AN IDIOT. I ACTUALLY *KNOW* MY SISTER'S NAME.

SO WHAT'S SHE DONE *THIS* TIME?

I'VE RECEIVED A REPORT-- *UNCONFIRMED,* MIND YOU--THAT SHE'S GONE MISSING. SHE'S POSSIBLY THE VICTIM OF VIOLENCE.

WHAT?

HOW?

HER *BOYFRIEND* WAS JUST HERE TO REPORT THAT HE'D FOUND HER APARTMENT *TRASHED* THIS MORNING.

OH, IS *THAT* ALL?

THANK YOU FOR NOT SMOKING

SNOW WHITE DIRECTOR OF OPERATIONS

"YOU HAD ME **SCARED** FOR A MINUTE, MISTER **WOLF,** BUT MY SISTER IS THE LAST OF THE **DEDICATED PARTY** FIENDS. SHE'S THE **ORIGINAL** WILD CHILD.

"FROM WHAT **I** HEAR, HER APARTMENT GETS TRASHED WITH ALARMING **REGULARITY.**"

I'M AFRAID **THIS** TIME IT'S DIFFERENT. I UNDERSTAND THERE'S BLOOD. **LOTS** OF IT.

I'M GOING OVER THERE NOW TO **INVESTIGATE,** BUT I THOUGHT YOU'D WANT TO KNOW RIGHT AWAY.

DAMNED **RIGHT** I WANT TO KNOW. I'M GOING **WITH** YOU.

I **DON'T** THINK THAT WOULD BE A GOOD IDEA. NOT UNTIL I'VE GOTTEN A FIRST-HAND **LOOK** AT THE SITUATION.

I'M NOT MUCH INTERESTED IN WHAT **YOU** THINK **IS** AND **ISN'T** A GOOD IDEA. SHE'S **MY** SISTER, I'M **YOUR** BOSS.

I'M **GOING** WITH YOU.

BOSS OR NOT, SNOW, I'M NOT ABOUT TO LET YOU INTERFERE WITH MY WORK. I TOLD YOU THIS AS A **COURTESY,** BUT I WON'T HAVE AN **AMATEUR** STAMPING THROUGH A POSSIBLE CRIME SCENE, DESTROYING **EVIDENCE.**

THEN WE SEEM TO BE AT AN **IMPASSE.** I SUGGEST A **COMPROMISE,** AND THE COMPROMISE IS **THIS:** I'M COMING WITH YOU, AND IF YOU DON'T LIKE IT, CLEAN OUT YOUR OFFICE AND GET OUT OF THE BUILDING.

HOW'S **THAT?**

OH!

OH MY!

YES! JUST LIKE *THAT!*

DO MORE OF *THAT!*

TRICK OR TREAT

YOU'RE *AMAZING.*

I KNOW.

I'VE ALWAYS BELIEVED A TRULY ACCOMPLISHED NOBLEMAN SHOULD HONE HIS COCKSMANSHIP EVERY BIT AS MUCH AS HIS SWORDSMANSHIP.

IN EACH CASE ONE SHOULD KNOW WHEN IT'S BETTER TO THRUST OR PARRY OR BIND.

WHEN IT'S TIME TO WITHDRAW OR RIPOSTE.

I DON'T KNOW WHAT *RIPOSTE* MEANS, BUT DON'T YOU DARE WITHDRAW YET!

AND OF COURSE, WHEN IT'S TIME TO FINALLY COMMIT ALL TO THE--DEEP--LUNGE.

YIPPEE!

MY HERO.

18

SO WHY DIDN'T JACK STICK AROUND *AFTER* HE REPORTED THE CRIME?

YOU'RE NOT ALLOWED TO *SMOKE* IN THE CAB, SIR.

SIR?

I SENT HIM AHEAD TO *GUARD* THE CRIME SCENE. I DIDN'T WANT ANYONE MESSING IT UP BEFORE I GOT A LOOK AT IT.

YOU HAD *JACK* GUARD THE *CRIME SCENE?* ISN'T THAT LIKE ASKING THE FOX TO GUARD THE HEN HOUSE?

HE'S THE *ONLY* ONE I CAN TRUST TO KEEP THE SCENE SAFE, SINCE HE'S THE ONE WHO *DISCOVERED* IT. IF JACK WANTED TO ALTER THE EVIDENCE HE ALREADY DID IT *BEFORE* HE CAME IN TO REPORT THE CRIME.

AND IF *THAT'S* THE CASE, HE WON'T WANT ANYONE ELSE COMING ALONG TO FURTHER *ALTER* HIS ALTERATIONS.

KEEP THE CHANGE.

OH JOY, NOW MY MOTHER CAN GET THAT *KIDNEY* OPERATION SHE SO DESPERATELY NEEDS.

I *STILL* DON'T TRUST HIM. I DON'T UNDERSTAND *WHAT* ROSE SEES IN HIM.

I ALWAYS GOT THE IMPRESSION THAT YOUR OPEN *DISAPPROVAL* OF JACK WAS THE THING THAT ROSE FOUND *MOST* ATTRACTIVE IN HIM.

I WOULDN'T CHARACTERIZE IT AS "DRIFTING." ROSE SEEMS TO HAVE DEDICATED HER *LIFE* TO DOING WHAT-EVER WILL CAUSE YOU THE MOST PAIN AND *EMBARRASSMENT.*

TRUE ENOUGH, I SUPPOSE...

...ROSE AND I *HAVE* DRIFTED APART OVER THE YEARS...

YOU'RE GETTING A BIT *NOSY,* MISTER WOLF.

I CAN'T *HELP* BUT NOTICE THINGS, SNOW. I BELIEVE THAT'S WHY YOU *HIRED* ME AS FABLE-TOWN'S SHERIFF.

THERE YOU ARE.

EVERYTHING JUST THE WAY YOU LEFT IT, JACK?

HAVEN'T GONE BACK IN YET.

I DIDN'T WANT TO SEE IT A SECOND TIME. IT'S *HORRIBLE.* YOU'LL SEE.

JUST GET THE DOOR OPEN.

HOLD THIS. I'M GOING TO NEED MY SENSES *CLEAR*.

BOTH OF YOU STAY *HERE*.

DO *NOT* COME IN FOR ANY REASON.

IF SOMEONE COMES, CLOSE THE DOOR AND STAY OUT IN THE HALL.

THIS STAYS *STRICTLY* AMONG THE FABLE COMMUNITY. *NO ONE* LETS THE MUNDY COPS IN ON IT.

NO MORE HAPPILY EVER AFTER

WHAT ARE YOU *DOING*? WHY ARE YOU LOOKING AT THE *FLOOR*? YOU *SHOULD* BE LOOKING FOR ROSE! CHECK IN THE *BEDROOM* TO SEE IF SHE'S IN THERE!

I ALREADY CHECKED. SHE'S NOT HERE.

BOTH OF YOU SHUT UP AND LET ME WORK.

SHE'S MY SISTER!

JACK, IF SHE OPENS HER MOUTH AGAIN, PICK HER UP AND CARRY HER BACK HOME. IF SHE SCREAMS OR RESISTS, YOU HAVE MY PERMISSION TO KNOCK HER SENSELESS.

FINE. I GET THE MESSAGE. I'LL KEEP QUIET-- FOR NOW.

LAY ONE HAND ON ME, ASSHOLE, AND YOU'LL REGRET IT.

Crusin Love Songs

AH *HA.*

JACK, I'M TAKING YOU IN.

WHAT FOR?

DOES IT MATTER? LET'S CALL IT RESISTING ARREST.

BUT I DIDN'T!

YOU POWER-MAD FUCKSHIT!

SEE?

OW!

NOW I CAN ADD ATTEMPTED ASSAULT TO THE CHARGES.

YOU'VE OCCASIONALLY BEEN CLEVER, JACK...

...BUT NEVER SMART.

OW!

THIS IS ABUSE OF AUTHORITY! AND I GOT A WITNESS!

SHUT UP, JACK, BEFORE I THINK OF OTHER CHARGES TO STACK AGAINST YOU.

IS HE THE ONE?

WE'LL SEE.

NEXT: THE (UN)USUAL SUSPECTS

CHAPTER TWO:
THE (UN)USUAL SUSPECTS

In which our intrepid detective delves deeper into the mystery of the missing Fable, and a prince is reunited with his old lady love.

Written by **Bill Willingham**
Pencilled by **Lan Medina**
Inked by **Steve Leialoha**
Lettered by **Todd Klein**
Colored by **Sherilyn van Valkenburgh**
Separated by **Zylonol**
Cover art by **James Jean**
Assistant Editor **Mariah Huehner**
Editor **Shelly Bond**

FABLES is created by Bill Willingham

THE NEXT DAY.

THE WOODLAND. THE SECRET "CITY HALL" OF THE UNDERGROUND COMMUNITY KNOWN TO ITS MEMBERS AS FABLETOWN.

♪ FROG WENT A-COURTIN'-- ♪

♪ --HE DID RIGHT-- ♪

--UH-HUH.

GOOD MORNING, MISS WHITE.

GRAND DAY, ISN'T IT?

LOVELY.

AND IN THE WOODLAND'S SMALLEST STUDIO APARTMENT....

GET UP. IT'S MORNING. *I* NEED TO GO TO WORK AND *YOU* NEED TO GET OUT.

TODAY'S TRUCK UPSTATE TO THE FARM LEAVES IN AN HOUR AND *YOU'RE* GOING TO BE *ON* IT.

YOU CAN'T KEEP *SNEAKING* INTO THE CITY TO *CRASH* ON MY COUCH.

LEAVE ME *ALONE*, BIGBY! I'M STILL *SLEEPING*! I GOT IN LATE LAST NIGHT!

WHY NOT? YOU STILL OWE ME *BIG TIME* FOR DESTROYING MY HOUSE.

ANCIENT HISTORY.

AND ALL I DID WAS SCATTER A FEW BALES OF *STRAW*.

AFTER WHICH YOU TRIED TO MAKE *SUPPER* OUT OF ME. LET'S NOT FORGET *THAT* MINOR DETAIL.

SO?

HOW DOES THAT *TRANSLATE* INTO " I HAVE TO PUT YOU UP EVERY TIME YOU ESCAPE FROM THE FARM"?

BECAUSE, BY *STAYING* HERE, I'M A LIVING SYMBOL OF YOUR LASTING REDEMPTION. WHO CAN CONTINUE TO DOUBT YOU'VE *RE-FORMED*, AFTER ONE OF YOUR OLD ENEMIES, A SUCCULENT *PIGGY*, SURVIVES SLEEPING IN YOUR APARTMENT?

I *HATE* IT UP ON THE FARM, BIGGS. I'M A *SOPHISTICATED* PIG AND I BELONG IN THE CITY.

NEVERTHELESS, IF YOU LEAVE THE FARM *AGAIN*, I'M TURNING YOU IN. *OFFICIALLY*.

YOU WANT SOME BREAKFAST BEFORE I KICK YOU OUT?

WHAT ARE YOU HAVING?

HAM 'N' EGGS.

I TAKE IT ALL BACK. YOU'RE *STILL* A MONSTER THROUGH AND THROUGH.

IN MIDTOWN MANHATTAN--

--THE APARTMENT OF MISS MOLLY GREENBAUM, WHOM WE MET, ALBEIT BRIEFLY, LAST ISSUE.

♪♫ IN DUBLIN'S FAIR CITY, WHERE GIRLS ARE SO PRETTY-- ♪♫

--I FIRST SET ME EYES ON SWEET MOLLY MALONE. ♪♫♪

Sweet Molly— While you slept I dashed out to retrieve my luggage from the Port Authority baggage check. I dropped off a couple of suits with the dry cleaners downstairs. Be a dear and pick them up for me this afternoon before you go to work. Also, if you have a moment, can you do a load of laundry for me? Just the few items in my suit-case. Make sure to carefully follow the washing instructions on the labels. I helped myself to your spare apartment key and some money from your purse. I didn't want to wake you to ask, and knew you wouldn't mind. I'll be camping here with you for a few days, if it doesn't put you out too much. See you tonight!
                                    — Your handsome prince du jour

THE WOODLAND'S GARDEN. AN HOUR LATER.

I *THOUGHT* I'D FIND YOU OUT HERE.

I LIKE TO COME HERE TO THINK--WHICH I DO *BEST* WHEN LEFT ALONE.

I WON'T TAKE UP *TOO* MUCH OF YOUR TIME, BUT I HAVE A FEW QUESTIONS ABOUT THE STATE OF OUR INVESTIGATION. FIRST, DID *JACK* REALLY DO IT?

PROBABLY NOT. BUT I NEEDED AN *EXCUSE* TO HOLD HIM IN CUSTODY, WHILE I CHECK OUT A FEW THINGS. SO HE'S OFFICIALLY *GUILTY* FOR A DAY OR TWO. AND FOR THE *RECORD*, THIS ISN'T *OUR* INVESTIGATION. IT'S MY INVESTIGATION.

SO WHAT ACTUAL CONCLUSIONS DID YOU COME TO?

NOT MANY. THE BLOOD IS YOUR SISTER'S.

HOW CAN YOU BE SURE?

YOU CAN'T FOOL *THIS* NOSE.

WE CAN HAVE IT *LAB* TESTED IF YOU LIKE BUT THERE'S *ZERO* CHANCE THAT IT ISN'T HER BLOOD.

31

SO SHE REALLY WAS THE VICTIM OF *VIOLENCE?*

IT LOOKS THAT WAY.

IF NOT JACK, WHOM DO YOU SUSPECT? SHE PARTIED WITH THE *MUNDANES.* DO YOU THINK ONE OF *THEM* MIGHT HAVE--?

"A MUNDY WOULDN'T HAVE KNOWN TO LEAVE THAT *PARTICULAR* MESSAGE ON HER WALL. NOT UNLESS ROSE HAD *REVEALED* HER FABLE NATURE TO ONE OF THEM.

WHOEVER DID THIS IS ONE OF US. A *FABLE.*

NO MORE HAPPILY EVER AFTER

"BUT AS *NONCONFORMIST* AS SHE IS, I DON'T THINK EVEN *SHE* WOULD BREAK THAT RULE."

THEN *MY* MONEY SAYS JACK DID IT.

I ALWAYS *LIKE* SUSPECTING JACK. HE'S BEEN A PERPETUAL LOAD IN MY *PANTS* SINCE DAY *ONE* OF THE EXILE. BUT I HAVE NO CHOICE OTHER THAN TO GO WHERE THE *EVIDENCE* LEADS.

OF COURSE *THAT* WON'T KEEP ME FROM *QUESTION-ING* HIM TODAY.

I WANT TO BE WITH YOU WHEN YOU QUESTION HIM.

I SUSPECTED AS MUCH. ARE YOU GOING TO INJECT YOURSELF INTO *EVERY* FACET OF MY INVESTIGATION? DON'T YOU HAVE A *GOVERNMENT* TO RUN?

ROSE IS MY *SISTER.*

AND YET YOU'VE BEEN *ESTRANGED* FROM EACH OTHER FOR *YEARS.* THERE'S BEEN LITTLE LOVE LOST BETWEEN THE TWO OF YOU.

IF YOU THINK *THAT,* MAYBE YOU *SHOULD* ADD ME TO YOUR SUSPECT LIST.

I ALREADY HAVE.

IS THAT SUPPOSED TO BE SOME KIND OF A *JOKE?*

NO, MA'AM. I'VE *NEVER* HAD MUCH OF A SENSE OF HUMOR. WE CAN GET YOUR INTERVIEW OUT OF THE WAY NOW, IF YOU LIKE.

I CAN'T JUST NOW.

MY *EX* JUST CALLED AND *INSISTED* I MEET HIM FOR A LATE BREAKFAST AT THE EGGMAN. I'M GOING OVER THERE NOW.

HIDE YOUR *WALLET* FIRST.

ELSEWHERE...

IF YOU'RE GOING TO *ADVANCE*, ADVANCE LIKE YOU *MEAN* IT.

MR. *BLUEBEARD*, IF YOU'RE GOING TO *INSIST* ON CALLING ME *PRINCESS*, PLEASE DON'T DO IT IN THAT TONE OF VOICE.

YOU AREN'T BACK IN YOUR *GLASS SLIPPERS*, WALTZING AT A DRESS BALL. A *MODICUM* OF GRACE IS IMPORTANT, BUT YOU GET NO POINTS HERE FOR *DELICACY*, PRINCESS.

YOU MAKE IT SOUND LIKE A FUCKING *SYNONYM* FOR--I DON'T KNOW--

--A *TURD* SANDWICH.

WHEN DID *YOU* GET TO BE SUCH A *POTTY-MOUTH*? DID YOU TALK LIKE THAT BACK IN THE *HOMELANDS*?

IS THAT WHY YOUR HANDSOME PRINCE *DIVORCED* YOU?

COULD BE.

GOOD LUNGE, BUT YOU LET YOUR *POINT* DRIFT OFF TARGET.

34

I DIDN'T WANT TO RISK *SKEWERING* YOU.

THEN YOU'RE WASTING *MY* TIME AND *YOURS*. IN FABLETOWN, WE FENCE WITH REAL *BLADES* BECAUSE WE'RE TRAINING FOR REAL *BATTLES*.

YOUR *HUSBAND* FANCIED HIMSELF A DEFT HAND WITH A BLADE. IT'S A WONDER HE DIDN'T PASS ALONG ANY *USEFUL* SKILLS BEFORE HE SET YOU ASIDE. ON-GUARD POSITION, PRINCESS. *MY* TURN TO ATTACK NOW.

ARE YOU PURPOSELY TRYING TO BE SO *BOOR-ISH*? IS THIS SOME CRYPTIC ASPECT OF YOUR *TEACHING* STYLE?

COULD BE. DID YOU KNOW PRINCE CHARMING'S BACK IN TOWN?

OLD NEWS. *EVERYONE* KNOWS HE'S SCAMMING FREE EGGS OFF WIFE NUMBER ONE, EVEN AS WE SPEAK.

THE *REAL* NEWS IS WHAT HAPPENED TO ROSE RED. DID YOU *HEAR* ABOUT IT?

NO. WHAT--?

SHE'S *DEAD*--CARVED UP LIKE A CHRISTMAS TURKEY. AND *RUMOR* HAS IT THAT CREEPY *BOYFRIEND* OF HERS DID THE DIRTY DEED.

JACK?

YEAH, I *THINK* THAT'S HIM. I HEARD HE WAS DANCING *NAKED* IN BITS OF HER SKIN WHEN THEY CAUGHT HIM--

OW! WHAT THE *FUCK*--!

I'M *BLEEDING*, YOU SHIT! WHY'D YOU *DO* THAT?

BECAUSE THIS IS *SERIOUS* BUSI-NESS AND YOU WEREN'T PAYING ATTENTION. *THINK* ABOUT THAT BEFORE YOUR NEXT LESSON.

I AM THE EGGMAN DINER

THANK YOU FOR COMING ON SUCH SHORT *NOTICE.*

I WOULDN'T HAVE MISSED IT FOR THE *WORLD.* I'M *DYING* TO FIND OUT HOW YOU BURNED YOUR LAST BRIDGES WITH EVERY ROYAL IN EUROPE, AND WHO YOU'RE *SPONGING* OFF THESE DAYS.

IT'S COMFORTING TO DISCOVER YOUR VOICE HASN'T LOST ANY OF ITS *VENOM* OVER THE YEARS, LOVEY.

WHY DON'T YOU TELL ME WHAT YOU *WANT,* SO I CAN GET BACK TO WORK.

UNLIKE *YOU,* I HAVE RESPONSI-BILITIES.

YES, I'D *HEARD* THAT YOU WERE RUNNING THE ENTIRE SHOW OVER HERE NOW. AND THAT'S WHAT I WANT TO TALK TO YOU ABOUT.

FORGET IT. I'M *NOT* ABOUT TO USE MY OFFICE TO GET YOU OUT OF TROUBLE, OR HELP YOU CHEAT SOME UNSUSPECTING FABLE OUT OF HER *FORTUNE.*

NO NEED. I'VE THOUGHT OF A WAY TO *REPLENISH* MY LOST FORTUNE, *WITHOUT* CHEAT-ING ANYONE.

DO TELL.

I'VE DECIDED TO *AUCTION OFF* MY ROYAL TITLE, PLUS MY LANDS, ESTATES; THE ENTIRE PRINCIPALITY. I'M GOING TO PUT THE WHOLE PACKAGE UP FOR SALE ON ONE OF THOSE *INTERNET* SITES.

ALL I NEED *YOU* TO DO IS SPREAD THE WORD AMONG THE FABLE COMMUNITY, CONCEN-TRATING ON THE *RICH* ONES OF COURSE.

YOU'VE GONE *DOTTY*, SWEETHEART.

WHY WOULD *ANYONE* PAY GOOD MONEY TO BUY LANDS THAT HAVE FALLEN UNDER THE ADVERSARY'S *DOMINION*, OR A ROYAL *TITLE* THAT HAS NO *AUTHORITY* IN THIS WORLD?

THAT'S THE *BEAUTY* OF MY PLAN, SNOW. WHAT ARE WE, LESS THAN TWO WEEKS FROM OUR ANNUAL REMEMBRANCE DAY CELEBRATION?

THIS IS THE ONE TIME OF YEAR WHEN *EVERYONE* GETS NOSTALGIC FOR THE HOMELANDS, AND STARTS BELIEVING WE ACTUALLY HAVE A *CHANCE* OF WINNING THEM BACK SOME-DAY.

IF WE ACT *FAST*, SOMEONE WILL BUY EVERYTHING I HAVE TO SELL, JUST ON THE *OFF* CHANCE THAT WE DO GET TO GO HOME AGAIN.

POSSIBLY SO. BUT WHAT MAKES YOU THINK *I'D* DO ANY-THING TO HELP YOU? DON'T YOU REMEMBER *WHY* I DIVORCED YOU? YOU *SLEPT* WITH MY *SISTER*.

"THE MINX *SEDUCED* ME."

I'M LEAVING *NOW*, BEFORE I *SCREAM*. CRAWL BACK INTO THE BED OF WHATEVER MUNDY WHORE YOU'RE *CURRENTLY* SHACKING UP WITH AND LEAVE ME *ALONE*.

BY THE WAY, THE "MINX" IN QUESTION HAS GONE MISSING, UNDER *FRIGHTENING* CIRCUMSTANCES.

IT'S JUST OCCURRED TO ME THAT *YOU* BELONG ON THE LIST OF SUSPECTS--

"--AND BIGBY WILL WANT TO QUESTION YOU ABOUT THAT LATER."

THIS SHOULDN'T TAKE LONG, JACK.

TAKE ALL THE TIME YOU NEED. I WANT TO DO *ANYTHING* I CAN TO HELP FIND OUT WHAT HAPPENED TO ROSEY, AND CONVINCE YOU I'M *NOT* THE ONE WHO HURT HER.

I'M SO WORRIED... MY GOD, THERE WAS SO MUCH BLOOD. *TOO* MUCH. I'M AFRAID SHE MAY BE--

IT WON'T HELP TO START THINKING THAT WAY *YET*, JACK. RELATIVELY *SMALL* AMOUNTS OF BLOOD, SPREAD AROUND--

--CAN GO A LONG WAY.

UNTIL WE TEST IT *FORENSICALLY*, WE CAN'T KNOW FOR SURE HOW MUCH OF ROSE RED'S BLOOD WAS SPILLED IN HER APARTMENT.

I'VE ALREADY ARRANGED FOR THOSE TESTS LATER, BUT UNTIL THEN WE SHOULD *ASSUME* WE'RE LOOKING FOR A *LIVING* WOMAN.

OKAY. WHATEVER YOU SAY. YOU'RE THE SHERIFF.

YOU'VE BEEN ROMANTICALLY INVOLVED WITH ROSE FOR HOW LONG?

ALMOST FOUR YEARS NOW.

BUT NOT FOUR YEARS STRAIGHT.

EXCUSE ME?

"JUST ABOUT A YEAR AGO, YOU AND ROSE HAD A VERY *PUBLIC* FALLING OUT. THERE WERE FIGHTS, LOTS OF SCREAMING.

"IT *NEARLY* GOT TO THE POINT WHERE I WOULD HAVE HAD TO INTERVENE.

"IN FACT, IF I RECALL CORRECTLY, SHE ATTENDED *LAST* YEAR'S REMEMBRANCE DAY WITH SOMEONE ELSE. *WHO* WAS THAT AGAIN?"

"*BLUEBEARD.* BUT SHE ONLY DATED *HIM* TO MAKE ME *JEALOUS.*"

HE'S THE ONE YOU SHOULD QUESTION, YOU KNOW HIS REPUTATION WITH WOMEN. MAYBE HE GOT *MAD* WHEN SHE LEFT HIM TO COME BACK TO ME.

WE'LL GET AROUND TO HIM. BUT LET'S FINISH UP WITH *YOU* FOR NOW.

YOU KEEP AN APARTMENT HERE IN THE BUILDING, RIGHT?

RIGHT. BUT YOU HAVE YOUR **OWN** KEY TO ROSE'S PLACE AND YOU STAY OVER WITH **HER** MOST NIGHTS?

YEAH, USUALLY, BUT NOT EVERY NIGHT.

WHY NOT THE NIGHT BEFORE **LAST**?

I'M NOT SURE. I WAS OUT LATE WITH SOME FRIENDS AND I GUESS I DIDN'T WANT TO WAKE HER, SO I CRASHED AT **MY** PLACE.

FUNNY, BUT GRIMBLE DOESN'T **REMEMBER** YOU COMING IN, **LATE** OR OTHERWISE.

GRIMBLE WAS ASLEEP BEHIND THE SECURITY DESK, LIKE **ALWAYS**.

YOU'D BE **SURPRISED** HOW MUCH REGISTERS WITH HIM, EVEN WHEN HE'S SAWING LOGS.

YOU'RE ALWAYS TRYING TO BEAT THE **SYSTEM**, JACK. THERE WAS THE TIME YOU TRIED TO STEAL NUMBLIN'S SEVEN LEAGUE **BOOTS** TO WIN THE NEW YORK MARATHON.

THE **BOSTON** MARATHON. AT LEAST I TRIED TO DO IT **OUT** OF STATE, TO DIVERT ATTENTION AWAY FROM FABLETOWN.

I **KNOW** HOW TO KEEP THINGS SECRET FROM THE MUNDYS. I DON'T RUN WITH THOSE **FANATICS** WHO THINK WE SHOULD ALL COME OUT OF THE CLOSET.

AND WHAT ABOUT THE TIME YOU TRIED TO RAFFLE OFF THE MAP TO YOUR REMAINING **MAGIC BEANS**?

WHAT LAW DID *THAT* BREAK? I HAVE A *RIGHT* TO MAKE MONEY OFF MY OWN PROPERTY.

EXCEPT THE MAP WAS A *FAKE* AND YOU LOST THE BEANS *CENTURIES* AGO-- IF YOU EVER HAD THEM AT ALL.

BIG DEAL. SO I TRY TO PLAY A GOOD-NATURED *GAG* NOW AND THEN. SO *WHAT?* I'M A TRICKSTER BY NATURE, BUT I'M NOT *VIOLENT*.

NOT LATELY, BUT YOU *DID* GO THROUGH THAT RE-MARKABLY BLOODY *GIANT-KILLING* PHASE WAY BACK WHEN.

ALL OF WHICH HAPPENED *BEFORE* THE GENERAL AMNESTY, WHICH MEANS IT *CAN'T* BE BROUGHT UP AGAIN.

HE'S *RIGHT*, BIGBY.

OR DOES THAT *PROTECTION* ONLY APPLY TO GRANNY-GOBBLING *WOLVES* WHO DON SHEPHERD'S CLOTHING TO BECOME LOW-RENT *COPS* DURING THE EXILE?

WATCH YOUR SMART *MOUTH*, SONNY BOY.

STOP IT! *BOTH* OF YOU! YOU'RE ACTING LIKE THIS IS SOME PRIVATE *GAME*, BUT YOU'RE AVOIDING THE *ONE* QUESTION THAT I NEED ANSWERED.

JACK, IS MY SISTER *DEAD?* DID *YOU* KILL HER?

FEEL BETTER NOW?

NOT BETTER, BUT BACK UNDER *CONTROL* AT LEAST. INDULGING MY ONE *VICE* HERE HELPS. CHOCOLATE CURES ALL ILLS.

SIX FORTY-FIVE, MISS WHITE.

WHY DON'T YOU LET *ME* HANDLE THINGS FROM NOW ON?

NOT A CHANCE. I'VE HAD MY *ONE* LOSS OF COMPOSURE. YOU WON'T HAVE TO WORRY ABOUT FURTHER *EMOTIONAL* FITS FROM ME.

DON'T BEAT UPON YOURSELF SO MUCH, SNOW. SOMETIMES PITCHING A *FIT* IS JUST THE RIGHT WAY TO INTERROGATE A SUSPECT.

WHO DO WE SEE NEXT?

I THINK WE'LL TAKE JACK'S ADVICE AND GO SEE THE RECLUSIVE MISTER BLUEBEARD. HE STILL LIVES IN THE BUILDING, RIGHT?

SINCE IT WAS BUILT. DO YOU WANT ONE OF THESE?

I DON'T EAT SWEETS.

I'D *HEARD* BLUEBEARD WAS WELL OFF. SO WHAT'S HE DOING DOWN ON THE *FOURTH* FLOOR? WHY DIDN'T HE TAKE ONE OF THE BIGGER APARTMENTS HIGHER UP?

YOU'LL SEE.

KNOCK KNOCK

YES?

WE CALLED AHEAD. YOUR BOSS IS EXPECTING US.

VERY WELL. COME IN.

FOLLOW ME, PLEASE.

OH, *I* GET IT *NOW*. HE'S GOT HIMSELF ANOTHER ONE OF THOSE MAGICAL *BIG* SPACES WITHIN A *SMALLER* SPACE, LIKE YOUR OFFICE. HOW DID HE PULL *THIS* OFF?

HE WAS ONE OF THE *FORTUNATE* FEW TO GET OUT OF THE HOMELANDS WITH HIS RICHES.

AND HIS WHOLE BLOODY *CASTLE*, TOO.

THAT'S **NOT** WHY WE'RE HERE.

TAKE A LOOK AT THESE PHOTOS. THEY WERE TAKEN IN ROSE RED'S APARTMENT LAST NIGHT, AND ALL THAT BLOOD IS **HERS**.

OH DEAR.

ALL WE NEED TO KNOW IS **WHY** YOU KILLED HER.

WHAT? HOW **DARE** YOU!

WOLF!

HOW DARE I **WHAT**? SPEAK RUDELY TO A MASS MURDERER?

THAT'S WHAT YOU DO, RIGHT? YOU MARRY THEM AND THEN **GUT** THEM?

MISTER WOLF! THAT'S **ENOUGH**!

YOU ARE AN **IMPERTINENT** MAN. I DEMAND SATIS-FACTION!

FUCK YOUR SATISFACTION, I THINK YOU **KILLED** HER AND I'M READY TO **ARREST** YOU FOR IT **NOW**.

CONVENE YOUR TRIAL, SNOW. I'M CHARGING THIS POMPOUS *ASSWIPE* WITH ROSE RED'S MURDER. HE ISN'T COOPERATING. HE'S *REFUSED* TO ANSWER A SINGLE QUESTION.

YOU HAVEN'T *ASKED* ANY! I'M *WILLING* TO COOPERATE!

THEN QUIT YOUR FUCKING *DISSEMBLING* AND ANSWER! DID YOU *KILL* HER?

NO!

DID YOU *HARM* HER IN ANY WAY?

NO. NEVER.

WHERE *WERE* YOU THE NIGHT BEFORE *LAST?*

HERE. ALL DAY AND ALL NIGHT. I *SELDOM* GO OUT.

A YEAR AGO YOU WERE SOCIALLY *BUDDY-BUDDY* WITH ROSE. WERE YOU TWO *ROMANTICALLY* INVOLVED, OR WAS SHE JUST A *TROPHY* DATE FOR PUBLIC OCCASIONS?

ROMANTICALLY.

AND YOU GOT MAD WHEN SHE *DUMPED* YOU TO *SLUT* HER WAY BACK TO HER OLD BOYFRIEND?

NO, BECAUSE SHE NEVER *"DUMPED"* ME, TO USE YOUR OWN *CRUDE* VERNACULAR. WE'RE STILL TOGETHER, THOUGH WE'VE LEARNED TO BE *DISCREET* ABOUT OUR RELATIONSHIP.

"A YEAR AGO--AT THE REMEMBRANCE DAY GALA--ROSE RED AND I BECAME ENGAGED.

"FOR REASONS ALL HER OWN, SHE *INSISTED* ON KEEPING OUR ENGAGEMENT SECRET FOR ONE CALENDAR YEAR; A CONDITION TO WHICH I AGREED."

WELL, AIN'T *THAT* A BIG *KICK* IN THE PANTALONES.

IS HE TELLING THE TRUTH?

I DON'T KNOW.

OF **COURSE** I'M TELLING THE TRUTH. I'M NO LIAR, AND IN **THIS** CASE I CAN **PROVE** IT.

HOW?

BECAUSE WE FORMALIZED OUR ENGAGEMENT IN **WRITING.** I ASSUME YOU CAN VERIFY HER SIGNATURE?

YOU MADE MY SISTER SIGN A **CONTRACT** PROMISING TO MARRY YOU?

ONLY BECAUSE THERE WAS A **PAYMENT** INVOLVED. A YEAR AGO I PAID HER A CONSIDERABLE **DOWRY--** IF SUCH A TERM ALSO APPLIES TO A PAYMENT MADE BY THE PROSPECTIVE GROOM TO THE PROSPECTIVE BRIDE.

"ROSE RED WAS AND **REMAINS** MY FIANCEE.

"IF SHE HAS TRULY FALLEN VICTIM TO SOME VIOLENT ACT, I'M **PERSONALLY** DEVASTATED, AND WILL BE REVENGED."

BUT, FOR THE MOMENT, I'M OFFERING A REWARD OF A **MILLION** DOLLARS FOR THE DISCOVERY AND CAPTURE OF WHOEVER PERPETRATED THIS **FOUL** DEED!

NEXT: AN ACCOUNTING IN BLOOD!

49

CHAPTER THREE: BLOOD TELLS

In which the boys make a big mess, more blood is spilled, and a determination is made about a missing Fable.

Written by Bill Willingham Pencilled by Lan Medina Inked by Steve Leialoha

Lettered by Todd Klein Colored by Sherilyn van Valkenburgh Separated by Zylonol

Cover art by James Jean Assistant Editor Mariah Huehner Editor Shelly Bond

FABLES is created by Bill Willingham

THAT'S THE LAST LOAD, BIGBY. CAN WE GO NOW?

THE GREENWICH VILLAGE APARTMENT BUILDING OF THE (POSSIBLY) FORMER ROSE RED.

NOT A CHANCE, BOYS. HAULING ALL THIS CRAP UP HERE WAS JUST THE FIRST ACT. YOUR WORKDAY HAS BARELY BEGUN.

THE BIGGEST PROBLEM WITH MY INVESTIGATION IS THAT I DON'T KNOW IF I'M LOOKING FOR A LIVE WOMAN OR A CORPSE.

THE ONLY WAY TO DETERMINE THAT IS TO RECREATE THE BLOOD EVIDENCE. THAT'S WHAT YOU TWO ARE GOING TO DO THIS MORNING.

OKAY, SUPER SLEUTH.

THIS APARTMENT IS DIRECTLY BELOW ROSE RED'S, AND ITS FLOOR PLAN MATCHES HERS.

FIRST, YOU'RE GOING TO SET UP THIS JUNK TO *DUPLICATE*-- AS MUCH AS POSSIBLE--HER FURNITURE LAYOUT.

THEN COMES THE FUN PART I PROMISED. YOU GET TO MAKE A BIG MESS.

USING THESE PRE-MEASURED PACKETS OF *BLOOD*, YOU'RE GOING TO RECREATE THE SPATTER PATTERNS OF THE APARTMENT ABOVE.

COOL.

"KEEP AN *EXACT* COUNT OF HOW MUCH BLOOD YOU HAVE TO USE TO MATCH THE SCENE UPSTAIRS. THEN WE'LL KNOW HOW MUCH OF ROSE RED'S BLOOD WAS ACTUALLY SPILLED.

"USE THESE PHOTOS FROM THE REAL CRIME SCENE TO MAKE YOUR RE-CREATION AS ACCURATE AS POSSIBLE.

"IF YOU ABSOLUTELY *HAVE* TO, YOU CAN GO UP TO CHECK OUT THE ACTUAL SCENE, BUT DON'T TRAMP ALL OVER THE EVIDENCE. AND GOD HELP YOU IF YOU LET ANY MUNDY SEE ANYTHING, OR IF YOU FORGET TO LOCK UP AFTER YOURSELVES.

YOU NEED TO GET MORE ON THE LOWER SHELVES, FLYCATCHER.

"BOY BLUE'S IN CHARGE. CALL ME AT MY OFFICE WHEN YOU'RE DONE."

THE WOODLAND BUILDING ON THE UPPER WEST SIDE.

YOU WANTED TO SEE ME, YOUR HONOR?

THE PENTHOUSE RESIDENCE OF KING COLE, UNOFFICIAL MAYOR-FOR-LIFE OF FABLETOWN.

OH, WE DON'T NEED TO STAND ON *FORMALITIES*, SNOW, NOT WHEN IT'S JUST YOU AND ME. COME IN.

THANK YOU, SIR. WHAT CAN I DO FOR YOU THIS MORNING?

I'M *TROUBLED* BY THIS UNFORTUNATE SITUATION WITH YOUR SISTER. TRAGIC, *AWFUL* BUSINESS. I UNDERSTAND YOU'RE ASSISTING BIGBY WITH HIS INVESTIGATION.

YES, SIR. I KNOW IT'S NOT THE *NORMAL* WAY OF THINGS, BUT IN THIS CASE I THOUGHT IT WAS *APPROPRIATE*, CONSIDERING SHE'S MY...

YES, OF *COURSE*. NO TROUBLE THERE. *ENTIRELY* UNDERSTANDABLE. BLOOD RELATIONS NEED TO LOOK AFTER EACH OTHER. WE CAN LET *OTHER* BUSINESS SLIDE FOR A DAY OR TWO, ONLY...

SIR?

I RECEIVED A *CALL* LAST NIGHT.

COMPLAINT, ACTUALLY. BLUEBEARD. BIG ANNUAL DONOR. COMMUNITY LEADER.

CLAIMS YOU AND MISTER WOLF ACCUSED HIM. *MURDER.* BURST IN ON HIM, SCREAMING AND SHOUTING.

TO BE *ACCURATE,* WE DIDN'T BURST IN ON HIM. BLUEBEARD *INVITED* US IN. BUT THE REST IS TRUE. BIGBY *DID* ACCUSE HIM, RATHER *LOUDLY,* OF MURDER.

WHY?

I HAVE NO *IDEA.* IT CAME OUT OF THE BLUE. IN FACT, HE DID THE SAME THING WITH JACK OF THE TALES. SO FAR AS *I* CAN TELL, BIGBY'S SOLE INVESTIGATION *STRATEGY* SEEMS TO CONSIST OF GOING FROM SUSPECT TO SUSPECT AND *ACCUSING* THEM.

DO YOU THINK HE MAY BE IN OVER HIS *HEAD?* AFTER ALL, HE WASN'T A *DETECTIVE* IN THE OLD LANDS. A BEAST OF THE MOST *UNRULY* SORT. *KILLER.* IS THIS JOB TOO MUCH FOR HIM?

WHO'S TO SAY? SO FAR HE'S BEEN THE *POSTER CHILD* FOR REFORM.

HIS RECORD'S BEEN SPOTLESS SINCE THE GENERAL AMNESTY. AND I DON'T KNOW ENOUGH ABOUT THE DETECTIVE RACKET TO FAIRLY *EVALUATE* HIS PERFORMANCE.

"SO FAR, MORE OR LESS IN ORDER, WE'VE TALKED TO *JACK*. AS HER CURRENT BOYFRIEND, HE WAS OUR FIRST *OBVIOUS* CHOICE FOR THE PERPETRATOR."

I'M *INNOCENT!*

"HE CLAIMS NOT TO KNOW ANYTHING ABOUT ROSE'S DISAPPEARANCE, BUT I'M NOT SO SURE. ONCE A ROGUE, *ALWAYS* A ROGUE. CURRENTLY, BIGBY HAS HIM COOLING HIS HEELS IN THE BASEMENT DETENTION CELL."

YOU MAY NOT HAVE DONE ANYTHING *THIS* TIME, JACK, BUT YOU WERE NEVER INNOCENT.

"THEN WE INTERVIEWED *BLUEBEARD*. YOU'VE ALREADY *HEARD* HOW WELL *THAT* WENT. MY GUESS IS BIGBY ACCUSED HIM JUST TO SHAKE HIM OUT OF THAT SUPERIOR, *ARISTO* POSE HE ALWAYS AFFECTS AROUND US *LOWLY* CIVIL SERVANTS."

HOW *DARE* YOU TREAT ME IN SUCH A FASHION!

BOO-FUCKING-HOO.

"IT *WORKED*. BLUEBEARD SURPRISED US WITH A DOCUMENT THAT APPARENTLY *PROVES* HE'S CONTRACTUALLY *ENGAGED* TO MARRY ROSE SHORTLY AFTER REMEMBRANCE DAY. I *DEARLY* HOPE IT'S A FAKE BECAUSE, AMNESTY OR *NOT*, I CAN'T *BLITHELY* FORGET WHAT HAPPENED TO EACH OF HIS PAST WIVES."

WHY WOULD I *KILL* HER WHILE WE'RE CURRENTLY *HAPPILY* BETROTHED?

"OUR THEORY WITH *HIM* IS THAT HE GOT *JEALOUS* WHEN ROSE DUMPED HIM TO GO BACK TO JACK, SO HE DID HIS TRADEMARK HORRIBLE THING TO HER."

BUT THE PROBLEM WITH *THAT* SCENARIO IS THAT, IN THE PAST, HIS *M.O.* WAS TO KILL THEM ONLY *AFTER* WEDDING THEM. ON THEIR WEDDING *NIGHT*, IN FACT.

"THEN WE DROPPED IN TO SEE THE **BLACK FOREST WITCH**."

I'VE BEEN GOOD, GAFFER WOLF.

YEAH. YOUR RECORD'S BEEN **CLEAN** SINCE YOU CAME TO TOWN.

BUT I CAN'T HELP BUT **WONDER** IF YOU HAVEN'T TURNED BACK TO YOUR OLD **EATING HABITS**.

WHAT DO YOU SAY, **GRANNY?** GROWING **TIRED** OF THE TASTE OF **GINGERBREAD?**

"WE CAUGHT UP WITH MY EX-HUSBAND, PRINCE CHARMING, LAST NIGHT IN THE **BRANSTOCK TAVERN.** BIGBY TOOK HIM ASIDE, SO I DIDN'T HEAR THE CONVERSATION. BUT IT DIDN'T LOOK ALL THAT **FRIENDLY.**"

YOUR PAMPERED **LIFESTYLE** BEGAN TO GO DOWNHILL SHORTLY AFTER SNOW CAUGHT YOU IN BED WITH HER SISTER.

WE **BOTH** KNOW YOU'RE TOO MUCH OF A NARCISSISTIC ASSHOLE TO EVER BLAME **YOURSELF** FOR ANY OF YOUR MANY FAILINGS, SO DID YOU BLAME **ROSE?** HAVE YOU BEEN NURSING A **GRUDGE** AGAINST HER FOR ALL THESE YEARS?

SHE **DISAPPEARED** A FEW DAYS AFTER YOU GOT BACK INTO TOWN. NICE **COINCIDENCE,** HUH?

YOU ARE A TEDIOUS, SMALL MAN, AND IN NEED OF MORE FREQUENT **BATHING.**

AND SOONER OR LATER, KING COLE, YOU'RE GOING TO FIND OUT THAT BIGBY CONSIDERS *ME* A SUSPECT AS WELL.

HE GOT MY INTERVIEW OUT OF THE WAY LATE LAST NIGHT.

"I HAVE NO IDEA IF HE DECIDED ANYTHING AS A RESULT OF IT."

YOU AND YOUR SISTER HAVEN'T BEEN FRIENDS FOR A LONG TIME.

WHICH HAS BEEN *PUBLIC KNOWLEDGE* FOR YEARS. IF I *REALLY* HATED HER ENOUGH TO KILL HER, WHY WOULD I WAIT UNTIL *NOW* TO ACT ON IT?

BECAUSE UNTIL *RECENTLY,* YOU WEREN'T THE NUMBER TWO AUTHORITY IN THE FABLETOWN GOVERN-MENT, AND ABLE TO THROW YOUR *WEIGHT* AROUND TO COVER YOUR TRACKS.

AGAINST *MY* WISHES, YOU'VE *INSERTED* YOURSELF INTO MY INVESTIGATION, AND YOU HAVE THE POWER TO *FIRE* ME IF I GET TOO CLOSE. NOT A BAD ADVANTAGE FOR A *MURDERER* TO HAVE.

TRUE ENOUGH. AND I'LL KEEP THAT IN MIND IF I EVER *DO* DECIDE TO KILL ANY-ONE.

"FINALLY, BIGBY SAID WE SHOULD KEEP *THE AD-VERSARY* IN MIND. HIS BLOODY CONQUEST OF THE FABLE REALMS MAY NOT HAVE ENDED AFTER SOME OF US WERE ABLE TO ESCAPE TO THE MUNDY WORLD.

"MAYBE SOME OF HIS AGENTS HAVE *FOLLOWED* US INTO EXILE, TO CONTINUE HIS WAR AGAINST US?"

BAD BUSINESS, MISS WHITE. *HORRIBLE* TO CONTEMPLATE. BUT STILL, IN THE FACE OF SUCH *TRAGEDY*, WE MUST CONSIDER *OTHER* MATTERS, TOO.

REMEMBRANCE DAY IS ALMOST UPON US AGAIN. HAVE TO CONSIDER THAT *TOO*, RIGHT? ANY WAY TO HAVE THIS MESS CLEARED UP BY THEN?

I COULDN'T SAY...

FABLETOWN IS OUR *FIRST* RESPONSIBILITY, YOU AND ME. IT'S ALL ON *OUR* SHOULDERS. IT'S A *NOBLE* EXPERIMENT, BUT *FRAGILE*. TENUOUS. MADE UP OF A DOZEN FACTIONS AND HUNDREDS OF OLD GRUDGES.

IT COULD *EASILY* COME APART OVER THIS INCIDENT.

I *REALIZE* THAT, SIR, BUT...

REMEMBRANCE DAY IS *MORE* THAN A BIG PARTY. IT'S WHEN WE GET MOST OF OUR *CONTRIBUTIONS* -- OUR OPERATING *BUDGET* FOR THE NEXT YEAR.

AND WALLETS *CLOSE* TO THE EXTENT THAT *CON-FIDENCE* IN OUR TINY GOVERNMENT *DIMINISHES*. UNDERSTAND?

I BELIEVE SO.

OF *COURSE* YOU DO. YOU'RE SMART. *COMPETENT*. YOU FIGURE THINGS OUT. DO WHAT YOU NEED TO, BUT HAVE THIS WRAPPED UP BY THE GALA.

I'M READY. THE *TRAY*, PLEASE.

GOT IT. THANK YOU. NOW, IF YOU'LL GET THE *DOOR*?

GOOD HUNTING, SIR.

KING COLE SURPRISED ME.

HE MANAGED TO HOLD OUT FOR TWO WHOLE *DAYS* BEFORE PUTTING PRESSURE ON ME TO GET THIS CASE SETTLED.

WHERE DID YOU GET ALL *THAT?*

FROM JACK'S APARTMENT. I JUST FINISHED *TOSSING* IT. IT WAS FULL OF COMPUTERS, AT LEAST SIX COMPLETE SYSTEMS. I *BORROWED* ONE SO THAT YOU CAN SNOOP THROUGH IT AND MAYBE FIGURE OUT WHAT HE'S DOING WITH THEM.

WHY *ME?* WHY DON'T *YOU* DO IT?

BECAUSE I CAN'T *USE* THE DAMNED THINGS. MACHINES *HATE* ME. I'M A GENETIC LUDDITE, INCAPABLE OF OPERATING ANYTHING MORE COMPLEX THAN MY TOASTER.

AND WHAT ARE *YOU* GOING TO BE DOING WHILE I'M DOING *YOUR* WORK *FOR* YOU?

THIS AND THAT. IT'S ABOUT JACK'S *LUNCHTIME*, SO I'LL SEE TO IT. AND I *STILL* HAVE A FEW NAGGING DETAILS TO FIGURE OUT ABOUT THE CASE.

IMPLYING THAT YOU'VE ALREADY *SOLVED* MOST OF IT?

YUP. I SOLVED THE BULK OF IT WITHIN THE FIRST *HOUR*. I PRETTY MUCH KNOW *WHAT* HAPPENED, AND MOST OF *HOW*, BUT I'M STILL SHORT ON SOME OF THE *WHO* AND *WHY*.

AND WHEN *EXACTLY* ARE YOU PLANNING TO CLUE *ME* IN?

THE VERY MOMENT I'M CONVINCED YOU AREN'T THE *VILLAIN* IN THIS MYSTERY.

AT *LEAST* TELL ME IF SHE'S DEAD OR ALIVE.

WE'LL SEE.

YOU CAN BE ONE *FRUSTRATING* SON OF A BITCH!

LITERALLY, IN *MY* CASE, BUT SHE WAS NEVER LESS THAN LOVING AND NURTURING. THE BEST *MOTHER* ANY BOY COULD WANT.

WHEN ARE YOU PLANNING TO SEE THE LOVELY PRINCE CHARMING AGAIN?

NEVER WOULD BE NICE. WHY?

BECAUSE I WANT YOU TO HELP HIM SELL HIS *TITLE*, BUT NOT *QUITE* IN THE WAY HE HAS IN MIND.

WHY WOULD YOU CARE ABOUT *THAT*? WHAT ARE YOU *UP* TO?

A MAD BUT *IMPROBABLE* SCHEME TO MAKE EVERYTHING COME OUT RIGHT IN THE END, WITHOUT ANY *FURTHER* BLOOD-SHED. AND JUST *MAYBE* THE FABLE COMMUNITY DOESN'T DISINTEGRATE IN THE PROCESS.

PROBABLY WON'T WORK, THOUGH.

AND IN ROSE RED'S APARTMENT BUILDING...

NO, FLYCATCHER. PAY *ATTEN- TION*.

HAPP*ILY*, NOT HAPP*ENING*.

HAPPILY: AITCH-AY-PEE-PEE-EYE-EL-WHY.

NO MORE *HAPPILY* EVER AFTER.

"NO MORE *HAPPENING* EVER AFTER" MAKES NO SENSE. NOT EVEN FOR A GUY WHO EATS *BUGS* FOR LUNCH.

I SLIP UP AND EAT ONE OR TWO FLIES, AFTER A HUNDRED YEARS OF NORMAL, *HUMAN* EATING HABITS, AND I'M BRANDED FOR *LIFE*.

PERFECT!

I THINK WE'RE DONE. I THINK WE DID IT.

SO HOW MUCH BLOOD DID WE USE?

IN THE LOBBY OF THE WOODLAND.

ONLY FIVE DAYS UNTIL *Remembrance Day.* HAVE YOU MADE YOUR RESERVATIONS YET? CALL 555-1234.

WAKE UP, GRIMBLE.

SORRY TO INTERRUPT YOUR FIRST IN A *GRUELING* SCHEDULE OF DAILY NAPS, BUT I NEED THE KEYS TO THE DETENTION CELL.

WHY?

IT'S TIME TO FEED THE PRISONER.

AGAIN? ARE YOU TRYING TO FATTEN HIM UP FOR THE *SLAUGHTER?* IF YOU'RE GOING TO TREAT PRISONERS *THIS* WELL, I VOLUNTEER TO BE YOUR *NEXT* ONE.

WHAT ARE YOU TALKING ABOUT?

HIGH LORD MUCKY-MUCK JUST BROUGHT YOUR *BOY* A BIG DAMN MEAL NOT TEN MINUTES AGO. GARLIC ROASTED *HEN,* IF MY NOSE HASN'T STARTED LYING TO ME.

WHO WAS IT?

BLUEBEARD, HIS OWN ROYAL SELF. *THAT'S* WHO. HE SAID YOU *AUTHORIZED* IT.

IN ANY CASE, IF YOU WANT THE *KEYS,* YOU'RE GOING TO HAVE TO GET THEM FROM HIM, BECAUSE HE AIN'T *RETURNED* THEM YET.

DAMN IT!

BILLY BEE HAMBURGER

I DIDN'T **DO** ANYTHING TO HER!

YOU MIGHT AS WELL TELL ME EVERYTHING **NOW**, BOY. I'M CONTENT TO CUT AT YOU ALL **DAY** AND ALL **NIGHT**, UNTIL YOU CONFESS.

TALK **NOW** AND YOU CAN SAVE YOURSELF SOME **PAIN**.

DROP THE **KNIFE** AND BACK **AWAY** FROM THE BOY--

PICK UP MY SHOES, JACK.

HAS IT ESCAPED YOUR NOTICE I'M *BLEEDING?* I NEED A DOCTOR.

POOR BABY.

WHOA!

YIKES!

WHERE'S THE *FIRE*, KIDS?

WE'RE COMING TO YOUR RESCUE.

MY *HERO.*

SOMEONE GET ME A *DOCTOR.* I'M *BLEEDING TO DEATH!*

CALM DOWN, JACK. YOU'RE FINE.

JOHN, WILL YOU AND GRIMBLE TAKE JACK UP TO USE THE FIRST AID KIT BEHIND THE DESK? AND THEN GET HIM TO HIS APARTMENT, AND MAKE SURE HE STAYS *PUT.*

WHERE'S BLUEBEARD?

HE **VOLUNTEERED** TO TAKE JACK'S PLACE IN CUSTODY. I HOPE HE LIKES THE CELL, BECAUSE HE'S GOING TO BE IN IT FOR A **LONG TIME**.

HE WAS IN THE MIDDLE OF **TORTURING** JACK WHEN I CAUGHT HIM.

WHY?

APPARENTLY HE BELIEVED SOME OF THE MORE **OUTRAGEOUS** RUMORS ABOUT WHAT ACTUALLY HAPPENED TO ROSE RED.

WHAT WERE YOU PLANNING TO DO WITH THE BIG **TOAD-STICKER**?

HELP YOU.

I'M **FLATTERED**, BUT GLAD YOU DIDN'T ARRIVE EARLIER, BLUE-BEARD IS EVERY **BIT** THE ACCOMPLISHED SWORDSMAN THAT YOU **AREN'T**.

HE MIGHT HAVE TAKEN THAT THING AWAY FROM YOU AND DONE BAD THINGS TO **BOTH** OF US WITH IT.

NOT BEFORE I GOT AT **LEAST** ONE GOOD CHOP AT HIM, AND THAT WOULD HAVE BEEN ENOUGH. THIS IS THE VORPAL BLADE OF **JABBERWOCKY** FAME. KILLS IN ONE **CUT**, SNICKER-SNACK AND ALL THAT? DOES ALL THE FIGHTING **FOR** YOU?

OH JOY, THEN DON'T *CARRY* IT THAT WAY, OR YOU'RE LIKELY TO CUT YOUR *OWN* HEAD OFF. I NEED YOU TO BE IN ONE PIECE FOR THE BIG PARTY NEXT WEEK.

EXCUSE ME?

WELL, I'D LOOK PRETTY DAMNED SILLY DRAGGING A *HEADLESS* WOMAN AROUND THE DANCE FLOOR.

WHEN DID *WE* DECIDE I'M GOING TO THE GALA WITH YOU? FOR THAT MATTER, WHEN DID *YOU* DECIDE TO GO? YOU *NEVER* GO TO THE REMEMBRANCE DAY CELEBRATION.

I CAN'T AVOID IT THIS YEAR. IF THERE'S *ANY* CHANCE TO WORK EVERYTHING OUT, I NEED TO BE THERE AND *YOU* HAVE TO GO AS MY *DATE.*

IT'S ALL VERY COMPLICATED AND I CAN'T EXPLAIN IT YET, SO JUST GO ALONG.

NOW, IF YOU'LL *EXCUSE* ME, I HAVE TO GO HOME AND CHANGE.

RINNNG RINNNG

KEEP YOUR *PANTS* ON! I'M *COMING!*

HELLO?

ZZZZZ

WHAT? OH YEAH. SORRY. I'VE BEEN OUT OF TOUCH FOR MOST OF THE DAY.

WHAT DID YOU FIND OUT? OH. OKAY.

SPY

DETECTIVE STORIES

NOT YET. I'VE GOT **MORE** BAD NEWS FOR THE TWO OF YOU. YOU NEED TO CLEAN UP THE PLACE. MOP, WAX, SCRUB AND PAINT UNTIL YOU RE-TURN IT TO **PRISTINE** CONDITION.

AND YOU NEED TO WORK **FAST**, BECAUSE WE COULD ONLY **AFFORD** TO RENT THE PLACE FOR TWO DAYS.

WHEN YOU'RE DONE WITH THAT, GO UP TO ROSE RED'S PLACE AND DO THE SAME THING, FROM TOP TO BOTTOM.

NOPE. I NO LONGER NEED TO **PRESERVE** THE EVIDENCE.

THEN, LAST OF ALL, TAKE THE RUINED FURNITURE FROM BOTH APARTMENTS OUT TO THE DUMP AND **BURN** IT.

AND DON'T LET THE **MUNDYS** CATCH YOU.

WHEN YOU'VE DONE ALL OF THAT, AND **ONLY** THEN, YOU CAN COME HOME.

YEAH, WELL MY HEART **BLEEDS** FOR YOU. YOU KNOW WHAT THEY SAY. THE ONLY **EASY** DAY WAS **YESTERDAY**.

HOURS LATER...

BIGBY. GLAD YOU WANDERED BACK IN BEFORE GOING TO BED. YOU WON'T *BELIEVE* WHAT JACK'S BEEN UP TO *THIS* TIME.

IT SEEMS OUR JACK IS THE SOLE OWNER OF *DREAM-WORLDZ.COM*.

SOME KIND OF ADVENTURE TOURS *STARTUP* COMPANY THAT HE'S BEEN TRYING TO TAKE *PUBLIC* FOR NEARLY A YEAR.

I WAS *HALF-WAY* HOPING YOU'D HAVE GONE HOME FOR THE NIGHT, SO THAT I COULD PUT THIS OFF UNTIL TOMORROW MORNING.

TRUST JACK TO TRY TO RIDE THE WAVE OF THE DOT-COM INVEST-MENT HYSTERIA ONLY *AFTER* EVERYONE'S FINALLY GOTTEN WISE TO THEM.

IT LOOKS LIKE HE LOST A *BUNDLE* WITH HIS LATEST GET-RICH-QUICK SCHEME.

SNOW, YOU NEED TO PREPARE YOURSELF FOR SOME BAD NEWS.

BUT *WHERE* DID JACK GET THE BUNDLE TO *LOSE*?

WHAT? *WHAT* DID YOU SAY?

THE AVERAGE ADULT FEMALE HAS A LITTLE MORE THAN NINE PINTS OF BLOOD. IRREVERSIBLE *SHOCK* OCCURS WHEN 40% OR MORE OF THAT VOLUME IS LOST.

I JUST HEARD THAT A *MINIMUM* OF FIVE PINTS OF ROSE'S BLOOD WAS SPILLED IN HER APARTMENT.

BUT...? NO, DON'T *SAY* THAT...

THAT MEANS THAT THERE'S *NO* HOPE THAT ROSE IS STILL ALIVE.

I'M SORRY.

NEXT: *WHODUNIT.*

AND JUST LIKE THAT, THE BIG DAY ARRIVED.

FABLETOWN'S GRANDEST EVENT OF THE YEAR, LIKE CHRISTMAS AND FOURTH OF JULY MULTIPLIED MANY TIMES OVER.

CHAPTER FOUR: REMEMBRANCE DAY

In which everyone dresses up to the nines, old stories are retold and the wolf takes a swim.

Written by
Bill Willingham

Pencilled by
Lan Medina

Inked by
Craig Hamilton

Lettered by
Todd Klein

Colored by Sherilyn
van Valkenburgh

Separated
by Zylonol

Cover art by
James Jean

Assistant Editor
Mariah Huehner

Editor
Shelly Bond

FABLES is created by Bill Willingham

AT THE FRONT DOOR BY TWILIGHT.

AS PROMISED, MY LOVE.

LADY BEAUTY, LORD BEAST, HOW **GRAND** YOU BOTH LOOK TONIGHT. AND I'LL BE A ROGUE IF YOU DON'T LOOK COMPLETELY **HUMAN** AGAIN, SIR. CONGRATULATIONS.

IT'S MY WIFE'S FAULT. SHE LOVES EVERYTHING ABOUT THIS DAY--INCLUDING **ME**, IT SEEMS--ENOUGH TO MAKE ME **HANDSOME** AGAIN.

DON'T START.

HERE YOU GO, JOHN.

OH NO, SIR, TICKETS ARE TAKEN AT THE *BALLROOM* DOOR, UP ON THE NINE-TEENTH FLOOR.

WHERE DO WE BUY THE *LOTTERY* TICKETS?

AT THE SECURITY DESK, MA'AM. JUST INSIDE.

COME ON, I WANT TO BUY A FEW MORE TICKETS BEFORE THE DRAWING TONIGHT.

WHY? THEY *COST* A BUNDLE THAT WE CAN'T *AFFORD*-- ALL FOR THE CHANCE OF WINNING A KINGDOM IN A PLACE WE CAN'T *GET* TO EVER AGAIN.

WIN A KINGDOM!

PURCHASE LOTTERY TICKETS HERE

WE ALREADY *HAVE* OUR OWN WORTHLESS LANDS AND CASTLE, LOST FOREVER IN THE HOMELANDS.

WHY GO INTO HOCK TO WIN *MORE* LOST LANDS AND *ANOTHER* USELESS TITLE?

KINGDOM CURE

BECAUSE THEY WERE *YOUR* LANDS AND *YOUR* TITLE. I WAS JUST A PEASANT GIRL WHO *MARRIED* INTO MONEY. I WANT SOMETHING OF MY *OWN*.

IF I WIN, I'LL BE A PRINCESS IN MY OWN RIGHT.

BUT STILL WORKING FOR MINIMUM WAGE IN A *BOOKSTORE*.

DON'T *SPOIL* THE EVENING, DARLING.

A HUNDRED DOLLARS A TICKET, BUT FIFTY DOLLARS *OFF* IF YOU BUY FIVE AT A TIME.

THIS IS *MARVELOUS*, SNOW. DO YOU SEE NOW WHY I NEEDED YOUR HELP? IT *NEVER* WOULD HAVE OCCURRED TO ME THAT THE BEST WAY TO SELL MY ROYAL TITLE WAS TO HOLD A LOTTERY.

ALL *SORTS* OF THINGS NEVER OCCUR TO YOU, DEAR. I SUPPOSE IT WOULD HAVE BEEN TOO MUCH TO EXPECT TO BE BORN *SMART* AS WELL AS PRIVILEGED.

OUCH.

HOW MUCH HAVE WE MADE SO FAR?

AS OF THIS MORNING, WE WERE CLOSING IN ON THREE HUNDRED *GRAND*, BUT SALES HAVE PICKED UP TODAY. I'D BE SURPRISED IF WE HAVEN'T *DOUBLED* THAT AMOUNT BY NOW.

LOVELY. WHO WOULD HAVE THOUGHT THAT SO *MANY* WOULD WILLINGLY SPEND SO *MUCH* FOR A SLIGHT CHANCE TO WIN ABSOLUTELY *NOTHING* OF SUBSTANCE?

NO WONDER THEY CALL LOTTERIES *TAXES* ON STUPID PEOPLE.

ARE YOU GOING TO ACT LIKE THIS ALL *NIGHT?* WHEN DID YOU FORGET HOW TO *ENJOY* YOURSELF? I SWEAR YOU'VE HAD THAT SAME *SCOWL* ON YOUR FACE FOR THE PAST THREE OR FOUR HUNDRED *YEARS.*

YOU OUGHT TO KNOW. YOU HELPED *PUT* IT THERE.

ISN'T THERE A STATUTE OF LIMITATIONS ON PLAYING THE POOR ABUSED *VICTIM?* WHY *DWELL* ON ONE UNFORTUNATE INCIDENT SO LONG AGO? YOU'RE LOVELY AND ETERNALLY *YOUNG.* MAKE THE *MOST* OF IT, SNOW BUNNY. MOVE ON.

IN FACT, TONIGHT YOU'RE AN *EXCEPTIONALLY* LOVELY WOMAN. DID YOU DRESS UP FOR ANYONE IN PARTICULAR, OR IS THIS FOR *MY* BENEFIT?

HONEY, IF WE DON'T HURRY UPSTAIRS, WE'LL MISS THE SACRED READING.

PARDON *ME,* BUT YOU'VE SUDDENLY GROWN WEARISOME AND *PEDESTRIAN.* I IMAGINE THAT WILL ONLY GROW *WORSE* AFTER TONIGHT.

DO *TRY* TO HAVE A PLEASANT FINAL EVENING AS A FORMER *SOMEBODY*--

--BEFORE YOU OFFICIALLY BECOME JUST ANOTHER *NOBODY.*

"ONCE WE WERE A THOUSAND SEPARATE KINGDOMS, SPREAD OVER A *HUNDRED* MAGIC WORLDS.

"WIZARDS OR WOODCARVERS.

"WE WERE KINGS AND COBBLERS.

"WE HAD OUR SINNERS, OUR SAINTS, AND OUR BLATANT SOCIAL CLIMBERS.

"AND FROM THE GRANDEST LORD TO THE LOWLIEST PEASANT GIRL, WE WERE, FOR THE MOST PART, STRANGERS ONE TO ANOTHER."

"BEYOND THE FARTHEST SHORES OF NEVER, THE ADVERSARY LIVED IN A REMOTE KINGDOM, IGNORED BY OTHER POWERS AS HIS STRENGTH AND AMBITIONS GREW OVER THE LONG CENTURIES.

"SOME SAY HE WAS A MERE WOODLAND SPRITE, WHILE OTHERS CLAIM HE WAS ONCE A GOD--

"--THROWN DOWN FROM THE VAST HEAVENS WHEN HIS CORRUPTIONS HAD BECOME TOO GREAT FOR HIS LOFTY BRETHREN TO TOLERATE.

"WHATEVER HIS TRUE ORIGINS, HE GREW INTO A DARK THING OF INFINITE HUNGER.

"AND AFTER HE'D CONQUERED HIS OWN LANDS, PUTTING EACH OF ITS FORMER KINGS TO THE SWORD, HE TURNED HIS UNQUENCHABLE APPETITES IN OUR DIRECTION.

"WHEN THE EMERALD KINGDOM FELL WE TISK-TISKED AND TUT-TUTTED IN OUR HOMES...

"...SAD FOR THE FATES OF THOSE UNFORTUNATE SOULS, BUT WE WEREN'T TEMPTED TO INTERVENE.

"AFTER ALL, THEY WERE ALWAYS ODD FOLKS, AND EVER SO FAR AWAY.

"IT WASN'T OUR BUSINESS."

"THEN THE KINGDOM OF THE GREAT LION FELL, AND AGAIN WE DID NOTHING, BECAUSE WE ALWAYS FOUND THE OLD LION TO BE A BIT TOO POMPOUS AND *HOLIER-THAN-THOU* FOR OUR TASTES.

"AND ONE BY ONE, OUR SCATTERED LANDS FELL UNDER THE ADVERSARY'S DOMINION, SWALLOWED UP INTO HIS EVER GROWING EMPIRE. HAD WE BANDED TOGETHER EARLY, WE *MIGHT* HAVE BEEN ABLE TO STOP HIM.

"BY THE TIME WE REALIZED THAT HE WASN'T MERELY INTERESTED IN CONQUERING *THAT* LAND, OR *THOSE* PEOPLE--THAT HE WAS COMING AFTER ALL OF *US*--IT WAS TOO LATE.

"HE'D GROWN TOO POWERFUL.

"MANY OF US DIDN'T HAVE THE *CHANCE* TO RUN."

"*SOME* OF US SURVIVED. TOO FEW. ALONE, OR IN SMALL GROUPS, OVER THE SPAN OF MANY YEARS--OF LIFETIMES-- WE HID AND RAN AND AVOIDED CAPTURE.

"WE LIVED AS OUTLAWS AND PHANTOMS.

"UNTIL WE COULD MAKE OUR WAY HERE, TO THIS DREARY MUNDANE PLACE: THE ONE WORLD THE ADVERSARY SEEMED TO TAKE NO INTEREST IN."

Until we could make our way here, to this dreary mundane place: the one world the Adversary seemed to take no interest in.
And here, united by our common enemy,
~~~~ old grudges We

AND *HERE*, UNITED BY OUR COMMON *ENEMY*, WE LEARNED TO SET *ASIDE* OLD GRUDGES. WE *FORGAVE* OUR MANY GRIEVANCES, TO MAKE *COVENANT* WITH EACH OTHER.

AND NOW, PREDATOR AND PREY, PRINCE AND PAUPER, WE ARE ALL OF A *SINGLE* COMMUNITY--

--ALLIED IN OUR UNDYING MEMORY OF THE HOMELANDS, AND THE *UNSHAKABLE* DETERMINATION THAT ONE DAY WE WILL RETURN TO *WIN* THOSE LANDS FREE OF THE *HATED* ONE.

"ELSEWHERE THROUGHOUT THE CITY, TONIGHT, IN PRIVATE HOMES...

"...AND TREASURED PUBLIC PLACES...

"...AND IN THE UPSTATE HOMES, WHERE OUR MORE INHUMAN MEMBERS DWELL...

"...OTHER GLASSES ARE RAISED, BY THOSE WHO COULDN'T BE WITH US HERE TONIGHT BUT ARE STILL CITIZENS OF FABLETOWN, AND ARE EQUALLY DETERMINED NEVER TO FORGET."

HI, PINOCCHIO. I HAVEN'T SEEN *YOU* IN A WHILE.

ENJOYING THE PARTY?

NO.

I AM MOST CERTAINLY *NOT* HAVING A GOOD TIME. I NEVER HAVE A GOOD TIME AT THIS RIDICULOUS CELEBRATION.

THEN WHY DO YOU COME EACH YEAR?

BECAUSE, SOONER OR LATER, THAT BLUE FAIRY, WHO TURNED ME INTO A *REAL* BOY, IS GOING TO SHOW HER FACE AT ONE OF THESE THINGS, AND I'M GOING TO KICK HER PRETTY AZURE ASS.

WHY? I THOUGHT YOU *WANTED* TO BECOME A REAL BOY.

OF *COURSE* I DID. BUT WHO *KNEW* I'D HAVE TO STAY A BOY *FOREVER?* THE DITZY BITCH INTERPRETED MY WISH TOO *LITERALLY.*

I'M OVER THREE CENTURIES OLD AND I *STILL* HAVEN'T GONE THROUGH PUBERTY.

I WANT TO GROW UP, I WANT MY BALLS TO DROP, AND I WANT TO GET *LAID.*

SECURITY OFFICE
B. WOLF

BOTH OF YOU, QUIT YOUR DAMNED BITCHING AND CRYING.

BUT WE'RE MISSING THE PARTY!

TRY TO GET IT INTO YOUR THICK SKULLS THAT YOU'RE NOT ONLY GOING TO MISS THIS REMEMBRANCE DAY CELEBRATION BUT THE NEXT ONE HUNDRED OF THEM TO FOLLOW.

I'VE GOT ENOUGH ON YOU TWO TO SEND YOU BOTH UP TO THE FARM FOR A CENTURY OF HARD LABOR.

BUT MAYBE THERE'S A WAY FOR ALL OF US TO AVOID THAT HARSH NECESSITY.

BULLSHIT, BIGBY! SURE, YOU GOT BLUE-BEARD HERE BECAUSE YOU CAUGHT HIM RED-HANDED TORTURING ME...

SHUT UP, YOU PATHETIC, BLEATING CHILD.

...BUT YOU'VE GOT NOTHING ON ME -- NOTHING YOU CAN PROVE, ANYWAY.

YOU'RE ABOUT TO FIND OUT EXACTLY HOW MUCH I CAN PROVE. BUT UNTIL I BRING THE HAMMER DOWN, YOU CAN BOTH GO TO WHAT'S LEFT OF THE PARTY--PROVIDED YOU STAY AT LEAST A DOZEN YARDS AWAY FROM EACH OTHER AT ALL TIMES.

BLUEBEARD, YOU'VE GOT JUST ENOUGH TIME TO CLEAN UP AND GET YOUR ANNUAL DONATION INTO OUR BELOVED MAYOR'S POCKET-- WHICH WILL REMIND US WHAT A GOOD AND SUPPORTIVE CITIZEN YOU ARE.

AND THIS TIME LEAVE THE GUNS, DAGGERS AND BATTLE AXES AT HOME, PLEASE.

AND JACK, WE'RE GOING TO TALK PRIVATELY FOR A BIT. THEN YOU'RE GOING TO DEMONSTRATE YOUR HELPFUL NATURE BY DELIVERING A MESSAGE FROM ME TO ONE OF THE PARTY GUESTS.

WHY DON'T YOU RUN YOUR OWN DAMNED ERRANDS?

"PARTLY BECAUSE I'VE *ALREADY* MISSED TOO MUCH OF THE PARTY, BUT *MOSTLY* BECAUSE THIS IS WHAT YOU HAVE TO DO IF YOU WANT TO KEEP YOUR FREEDOM."

NO NO *NO!* TOO MUCH *STIRRING!* THE SAUCE MUST BE *ALLOWED* TO CARMELIZE.

WHERE ARE MY CORNISH HENS? WHO *TOOK* THEM?

SHALLOTS? BUT YOU *CLEAR-LY* SAID RED ONIONG!

ARE WE STILL SERVING SOUP?

WE'RE ALMOST OUT OF THE GOOSE LIVER. SHOULD WE PUT OUT MORE OR--?

BETTER PUT OUT MORE OF SOMETHING *FAST.* THIS CROWD'S EATING ANYTHING IN SIGHT.

YOU HURRY UP AND YOU SLOW DOWN! *EVERY-THING* MUST BE COORDINATED TO ARRIVE AT THE *PROPER* TIME!

I FINALLY *MADE* IT.

BACKSTAGE AT THE *GRANDEST* EVENT OF THE YEAR.

YUM.

ARE YOU ON THE MENU?

OH GOSH. I SURE *HOPE* NOT.

THERE YOU ARE. DON'T YOU LOOK NICE.

I WAS *BEGINNING* TO THINK I'D BEEN STOOD *UP.*

NO MATTER. YOU ALWAYS GO TO THIS THING *STAG*, RIGHT?

SO IT'S NOT AS IF YOU'D SUFFER ANY *EMBARRASSMENT* IF I NEVER SHOWED.

MY GOD, ARE YOU *COMPLETELY* DEVOID OF SOCIAL SKILLS?

PROBABLY. COME ON, WE NEED TO BE OUT ON THE DANCE FLOOR.

WHY? IS THIS *ANOTHER* PART OF YOUR COMPLEX SCHEME TO CATCH MY SISTER'S KILLER?

COULD BE. NOW, SHOW ME HOW WE DO THIS.

YOU'VE NEVER *DANCED* BEFORE?

NEVER.

PUT YOUR HANDS HERE AND HERE. A LITTLE MORE *GENTLY*, PLEASE. I'M NOT SOME SUSPECT YOU'RE ABOUT TO WRESTLE TO THE GROUND. NOW, FOLLOW MY *LEAD* AND TRY TO STAY OFF MY *FEET.*

YES, DEAR.

LOOK UP.

THEN I CAN'T SEE MY *FEET*.

DO IT ANYWAY. YOU LOOK LIKE YOU'RE TRYING TO PEEK DOWN MY *DRESS*.

SO? WHY WOULD YOU WEAR A NECK-LINE LIKE *THAT* IF YOU DIDN'T *WANT* PEOPLE TO LOOK?

PERHAPS WOMEN *WEAR* LOW NECK-LINES TO FILTER OUT THE *GENTLEMEN* FROM THE DOGS. THOSE FEW WHO CAN STILL MANAGE *EYE* CONTACT, EVEN IN THE PRESENCE OF BREASTS LIKE THESE, MIGHT ACTUALLY HAVE SOME POTENTIAL.

WOOF.

OUCH. WATCH YOUR FEET.

BUT YOU JUST SAID *NOT* TO WATCH MY FEET.

OH MY, IS *HE* YOUR DATE, PRINCESS?

YOU *POOR* GIRL.

DON'T *LITERALLY* WATCH YOUR FEET, JUST *KINDLY* STOP STOMPING ALL OVER *MINE*.

GOT IT. SO HOW LONG DO WE HAVE TO DO THIS BEFORE WE EAT?

MISTER WOLF, YOU'VE GOT SOME *COOL MOVES!*

DON'T ASK *ME*. DANCING WAS *YOUR* IDEA.

A VERY *BAD* IDEA. I DIDN'T ANTICIPATE BEING...

"...THE CENTER OF SO MUCH ATTENTION.

CASE IN POINT. LET'S GO EAT. OR DRINK. LET'S GO DO *ANYTHING* OTHER THAN THIS.

OKAY, BUT YOU WERE SO *LATE* THAT MOST OF THE GOOD FOOD IS ALREADY GONE.

BUT DON'T WORRY.

I'M AN OLD *VETERAN* OF THESE AFFAIRS.

AND I'LL LET YOU IN ON A BIG *SECRET*. THE CATERERS ALWAYS *STEAL* THE BEST OF THE REAL DELICACIES FOR THEMSELVES.

THEY KEEP THE *GOOD* STUFF LOCKED AWAY IN THE BACK, THEN SNEAK IT HOME AFTER THE PARTY.

IF YOU LIKE, WE CAN RAID THE *KITCHEN* AND MAKE THOSE PIRATES *SURRENDER* A SHARE OF THE LOOT, IN EXCHANGE FOR NOT BLOWING THE WHISTLE ON THEM.

THAT'S *IT*.

WHAT'S *WHAT*?

YOU JUST *SOLVED* THE LAST NAGGING BIT OF THE MYSTERY.

DID I?

OF COURSE. ROSE WAS A *PARTY GIRL!* PEOPLE--FABLE AND MUNDY ALIKE--WERE IN AND OUT OF HER APARTMENT *CONSTANTLY,* OFTEN WHETHER SHE WAS THERE OR NOT. SHE PUT THE PADLOCK ON HER FREEZER TO KEEP ANYONE FROM GETTING AT THE *GOOD* STUFF.

SO FAR, I'M NOT FOLLOWING YOU.

IT WASN'T REALLY IMPORTANT, BUT IT WAS THE *ONLY* PIECE OF THE PUZZLE I COULDN'T WORK OUT. NOW IT'S FINALLY COMPLETE.

DO YOU WANT TO KNOW WHO KILLED ROSE RED?

OF COURSE!

THEN SPREAD THE WORD--DISCREETLY. ANYONE WHO'S INTERESTED IN WHAT HAPPENED, *AND* WHO DID IT, SHOULD HEAD UPSTAIRS TO KING COLE'S TERRACE--RIGHT AFTER THE LOTTERY DRAWING.

AND THE **WINNING** TICKET IS...

DOES HIS **ROYAL NIBS** KNOW YOU SNEAK UP HERE TO USE HIS **POOL** WHEN HE'S NOT AROUND?

WHO KNOWS?

IF HE **DOES,** HE'S NEVER COMPLAINED.

MIND IF I **BUM** A SMOKE?

I GUESS NOT.

DID YOU FINISH YOUR ERRANDS, JACK?

THAT'S **PRINCE** JACK TO YOU, COMMONER.

OH, NO, DON'T TELL ME...

YUP. I WON THE GODDAMN **LOTTERY**--AND I ONLY BOUGHT A SINGLE TICKET ON A LARK.

ISN'T THAT A KICK IN THE *NADS?* ALL MY LIFE I'VE BEEN TRYING ONE CRAZY SCHEME AFTER ANOTHER TO MAKE IT *BIG,* AND ALL I HAD TO DO WAS BUY A *TICKET.*

TOO BAD IT'S ALL *WORTHLESS.*

TRUE. WE CAN ALL *DREAM* ABOUT THE DAY WHEN WE'LL KICK THE ADVERSARY'S ASS OUT OF OUR OLD LANDS--INCLUDING MY *NEW* OLD LANDS NOW--BUT ANYONE WHO'S NOT A ROMANTIC FOOL KNOWS IT'S *NEVER* GOING TO HAPPEN.

READY TO BEGIN YOUR SHOW? IT LOOKS LIKE THE *RUBES* HAVE ARRIVED.

JUST REMEMBER TO DO YOUR PART ON *CUE,* YOUR "HIGHNESS."

THIS IS IT. IN THE MYSTERY NOVELS THIS IS CALLED THE "PARLOR SCENE," WHERE THE CLEVER *DETECTIVE* REVEALS ALL.

IF THIS WERE A WORK OF *FICTION,* THE AUTHOR WOULD PAUSE THE STORY *HERE* TO ASK THE READERS IF THEY'D PUT ALL THE CLUES TOGETHER YET.

OH *DO* GET *ON* WITH IT, YOUNG MAN.

SORRY, SIR, BUT IN OUR SECRET HEARTS EVERY *REAL* COP LONGS FOR A MOMENT LIKE THIS, AND *DAMN FEW* GET ONE. *INDULGE* ME, PLEASE.

JACK, WILL YOU ASK OUR VILLAIN TO *JOIN* US NOW?

ANYTHING YOU SAY, BWANA.

YOU'VE GOT HER *MURDERER* HERE?

YES, I SUSPECTED THE KILLER COULDN'T RESIST ATTENDING OUR ANNUAL BALL, AND I HAD JACK CIRCULATE AMONG THE GUESTS TO LOOK FOR HER.

HER?

WHO?

DO WE *HAVE TO DO* THIS?

ABSOLUTELY.

LADIES AND GENTLEMEN, I GIVE YOU ROSE RED'S *KILLER...*

ROSE RED.

HOW IN ALL THE HELLS?

I DEMAND AN EXPLANATION!

HOW DID YOU PULL A TRICK LIKE THIS?

ROSE!

BUT THERE WAS TOO MUCH BLOOD!

WHICH WE HAD TO CLEAN!

ROSE, WHY DID YOU DO IT?

IF YOU WEREN'T KILLED, THEN--!

AN INVESTIGATION!

ONE AT A TIME!

IF YOU'D ALL RETURN TO YOUR SEATS--

SIT DOWN, YOU GOOFS!

IT'S JUST A GIRL BACK FROM THE DEAD!

HOW DID YOU-- WHY WOULD YOU PUT US ALL THROUGH THIS?

IT'S NOT MY FAULT!

EVERYONE CALM DOWN, SIT DOWN, AND STOP TALKING FOR JUST A MOMENT--

--AND I'LL TELL YOU ALL WHAT SHE DID, HOW SHE DID IT AND WHY SHE DID IT.

NEXT: THE BIG REVEAL!

"DESPITE WHAT YOU SEE ON *TV*, THE TYPICAL COP'S LIFE CAN BEST BE DESCRIBED AS UNENDING *HOURS* OF MIND-NUMBING *DRUDGERY*.

"GUNFIGHTS AND CAR CHASES ARE FEW AND FAR BETWEEN. THEY GENERATE SO MUCH EXTRA *PAPERWORK*-- AND SECOND-GUESSING BY EVERYONE NOT INVOLVED--THAT NO *SANE* COP WELCOMES SUCH BREAKS IN THE GENERAL TEDIUM OF POLICE WORK."

AND NO *HONEST* COP EVER GETS *RICH*.

AT LEAST A MUNDY COP GETS TO *RETIRE* AFTER TWENTY TO FORTY YEARS.

I'VE BEEN ON THE JOB FOR MORE THAN TWO *HUNDRED* YEARS -- EVER SINCE THE FIRST DAYS OF THE FABLES IN EXILE COMPACT AND GENERAL AMNESTY.

SSSSTRRRCCHH

I'VE NEVER BEEN IN A GUNFIGHT--OR *FIRED* A GUN FOR THAT MATTER.

I'VE NEVER BEEN IN A CAR CHASE--MUCH LESS *LEARNED* TO DRIVE.

AND EVEN THE NUMBER OF TIMES I'VE HAD TO CHASE A SUSPECT ON *FOOT* CAN BE COUNTED ON ONE HAND.

CHAPTER FIVE:
The Famous Parlor Room Scene (Sans Parlor)

In which everything is neatly wrapped up in the end, even though few are satisfied with the outcome.

ALL IN ALL, I CAN'T SAY I'VE HAD WHAT COULD BE DESCRIBED AS AN *EXCITING* CAREER--OR EVEN A VERY *INTERESTING* ONE.

BUT *ONCE* IN A GREAT WHILE, SMALL REWARDS *DO* COME ALONG.

ANYONE WHO'S EVER FANCIED HIMSELF A DETECTIVE, OPENLY OR *SECRETLY*, LONGS FOR THE DAY HE CAN DO THE FAMOUS PARLOR ROOM SCENE.

WHAT THE HELL IS *THAT?*

IT'S THE MOMENT WHEN I GET TO REVEAL *WHO DID WHAT, HOW* THEY DID IT--AND MOST *IMPORTANT*-- HOW *I* FIGURED IT ALL OUT.

Written by
Bill Willingham
Pencilled by
Lan Medina
Inked by
Steve Leialoha
Lettered by
Todd Klein
Colored by Sherilyn Separated Cover art by
van Valkenburgh by Zylonol James Jean
Assistant Editor Editor FABLES is created
Mariah Huehner Shelly Bond by Bill Willingham

BUT WE ALL HAVE TO GO TO A *PARLOR* FIRST?

NO, FLY-CATCHER, THE ACTUAL *SETTING* DOESN'T MATTER. *THIS* WILL DO FINE.

THEN GET *ON* WITH IT, MR. WOLF. *TELL YOUR STORY.* I CAN'T TOLERATE THE *SUSPENSE.*

WHEN THE LORD MAYOR OF FABLETOWN *COMMANDS,* I CAN ONLY *OBEY.*

MY SUSPICIONS ABOUT THE *TRUE* NATURE OF THIS CASE WERE RAISED THE VERY *MOMENT* I FIRST LEARNED OF IT.

"WE'RE ON THE UPPER WEST SIDE, FAR AWAY FROM ROSE RED'S APARTMENT DOWN IN THE VILLAGE. JACK HAD TO TAKE A *CAB* UP HERE IN ORDER TO REPORT THE SO-CALLED *CRIME.*

"JACK'S IN PRETTY GOOD SHAPE.

"A SIMPLE RUN TO MY OFFICE, FROM A CAB PARKED OUTSIDE, SHOULDN'T HAVE *WINDED* HIM."

"BUT HE ARRIVED FRANTIC AND OUT OF BREATH."

...huh... huh...

A TERRIBLE *THING* HAPPENED!

WHY? BECAUSE HE NEEDED TO **SELL** ME ON THE FICTION THAT HE'D JUST DISCOVERED A HORRIBLE CRIME AND RUSHED RIGHT OVER TO REPORT IT.

AND, BEING **JACK**, HE OVERDID IT.

I TOLD YOU TO BE **SUBTLE**, JACKASS.

BUT--

YOU TWO STAY OUT IN THE HALL.

" SO, TIPPED OFF IN ADVANCE NOT TO TAKE **ANYTHING** AT FACE VALUE, I TOOK A LOOK AT ROSE RED'S APARTMENT.

NO MORE HAPPILY EVER AFTER

"WITHIN SECONDS IT WAS OBVIOUS THAT IT WAS A **STAGED** CRIME SCENE-- AND STAGED **BADLY** AT THAT."

"BLOOD WAS SPILLED AND SPATTERED EVERY-WHERE--ALL OVER EVERY SURFACE OF ROSE'S LIVING ROOM.

"NO ONE COULD HAVE GONE IN AND OUT OF THERE, AFTER THE VIOLENCE, WITHOUT LEAVING PLENTY OF FOOTPRINTS.

"AND YET JACK SAID HE'D SEARCHED THE PLACE, LOOKING FOR ROSE."

CHECK IN THE BEDROOM TO SEE IF SHE'S IN THERE!

I ALREADY CHECKED. SHE'S NOT HERE.

WHY COULDN'T IT BE THAT I WAS JUST CAREFUL TO SKIP AND HOP OVER THE BLOOD SPATTERS, LIKE YOU DID, TO PRESERVE THE EVIDENCE?

OH SURE. THAT MAKES PERFECT SENSE.

NOT A CHANCE, JACK. NO ONE ENCOUNTERING A SCENE LIKE THAT WORRIES ABOUT PRESERVING EVIDENCE WHILE HIS LADY LOVE MAY STILL BE IN THE BACK ROOM BLEEDING HER LIFE AWAY.

BUT THAT WAS FAR FROM YOUR ONLY AMATEUR MISTAKE.

THE NEXT TIME YOU TWO TRY TO STAGE A CRIME SCENE, YOU SHOULD ACTUALLY KNOCK THINGS OVER--

--RATHER THAN CAREFULLY PLACE THEM IN POSITIONS YOU WANT THEM TO END UP IN.

"THE POLE LAMP WAS KNOCKED OVER, BUT ITS LIGHT BULBS WERE STILL *INTACT*.

"ROSE RED'S FAVORITE HANDMADE CERAMIC ASHTRAY WAS *SUPPOSEDLY* KNOCKED TO THE FLOOR, WITHOUT SO MUCH AS *CHIPPING* IT.

"ROSE MUST HAVE WANTED TO PRESERVE HER STEREO SET, BECAUSE IT *MIRACULOUSLY* AVOIDED GETTING SPATTERED, EVEN THOUGH BLOOD WAS *LIBERALLY* SPLASHED TO EACH SIDE OF IT.

"SHE WANTED TO SAVE THE BEST OF HER MUSIC COLLECTION AS WELL.

"COMPACT DISKS SPREAD OUT ALL OVER THE FLOOR MAKE FOR GOOD SET *DECORATION*, WHEN ONE WANTS TO SUGGEST THAT A VIOLENT *STRUGGLE* HAS TAKEN PLACE.

"BUT SHE WAS ONLY WILLING TO SACRIFICE THE CD'S SHE *DIDN'T* LIKE SO MUCH-- THE ONES IN THE *BACK*-- TO SCATTER ON THE FLOOR.

" THE CD'S SHE PLAYED *MOST*-- THE ONES IN THE *FRONT*-- WERE UNTOUCHED."

SEE? I TOLD YOU WE SHOULD'VE USED SOME OF YOUR GOOD CD'S.

SHUT UP.

YOU MADE IT PRETTY OBVIOUS THAT ONE OR BOTH OF YOU EXPECTED TO MAKE FUTURE USE OF THE STEREO AND SUCH.

BUT ROSE WOULDN'T HAVE CONSIDERED THOSE THINGS WHILE FIGHTING FOR HER LIFE.

"YOU DIDN'T CARE ABOUT YOUR OLD, SECOND-HAND TOASTER, SO YOU USED IT TO ADD TO THE PICTURE OF CHAOTIC MESS.

"BUT UNTIDY AS IT WAS, YOUR KITCHEN WAS UNTOUCHED BY THE FICTIONAL STRUGGLE.

"SO HOW DID THE TOASTER MAKE IT FROM YOUR KITCHEN TO THE MIDDLE OF YOUR LIVING ROOM FLOOR?"

OKAY, WOLF, ENOUGH ALREADY WITH THE STEREO SETS AND TOASTERS.

YOU'VE IMPRESSED US ALL WITH HOW EASILY YOU SNIFFED OUT THE TRUTH.

BUT WHAT *I* WANT TO KNOW IS *THIS*: IF YOU KNEW FROM THE VERY BEGINNING THAT ROSE WAS STILL *ALIVE*, WHY DID YOU GO ON *PRETENDING* TO INVESTIGATE?

HOLD ON, TIGER. PULL YOUR *CLAWS* BACK IN.

HOW COULD YOU LET ME GO FOR DAYS-- WEEKS--

--THINKING MY SISTER WAS *DEAD*, WHEN ALL ALONG YOU KNEW SHE *WASN'T?*

PAY ATTENTION. I ONLY KNEW FOR *CERTAIN* THAT YOUR SISTER PARTICIPATED IN *STAGING* THE CRIME SCENE.

I DIDN'T KNOW SHE *WASN'T DEAD.* IN FACT, I HAD PRETTY COMPELLING EVIDENCE THAT SHE *WAS.*

BUT *YOU* SAID--

THERE WAS MORE *BLOOD* AT THE SCENE THAN ANY *ONE* PERSON COULD LOSE AND STILL BE *ALIVE.* AND I *KNEW* IT ALL BELONGED TO ROSE RED.

DISCOVERING THAT THE CRIME SCENE WAS *STAGED* WAS A *FAR CRY FROM* SOLVING THE ENTIRE MYSTERY.

"THERE WERE TOO MANY *POSSIBILITIES* TO FIT THE AVAILABLE EVIDENCE.

"ROSE COULD HAVE PLANNED IT TO MAKE HER *SUICIDE* LOOK LIKE A MURDER!"

"OR SHE *COULD* HAVE PARTICIPATED IN THE SCAM TO *FAKE* HER DEATH--

"--NOT REALIZING THAT HER PARTNER-IN-CRIME DECIDED TO MAKE IT A *REAL MURDER SCENE!*"

BUT IT WASN'T *EITHER* OF THOSE, OF COURSE. THE COPIOUS AMOUNTS OF BLOOD WERE THE *ONE* PART OF THEIR PLAN WHERE JACK AND ROSE HAD THOROUGHLY *OUT-SMARTED* ME--FOR A WHILE.

SNOW, YOU WERE THE ONE WHO GAVE ME THE FINAL *CLUE*--

--YOU HELPED ME FIT THE LAST NAGGING PIECES INTO PLACE.

HOW?

"EARLIER THIS EVENING, WHILE WE WERE DANCING AT THE GALA."

LET'S EAT.

TOO LATE. THE *GOOD* FOOD IS ALREADY GONE.

"YOU SAID SOMETHING ABOUT LOCKING THE FOOD AWAY TO KEEP THE PARTY GUESTS FROM GETTING TO IT."

BUT WE CAN *RAID* THE KITCHEN.

THE CATERERS *ALWAYS* KEEP THE GOOD STUFF LOCKED AWAY IN THE BACK.

THAT'S HOW THEY DID IT. THE AVERAGE PERSON CAN GIVE UP A PINT OF BLOOD EVERY SIX WEEKS WITHOUT SUFFERING ANY ILL EFFECTS.

"THEY **HAD** TO HAVE HAD THIS IDIOT SCHEME PLANNED FOR SOME TIME...

"...BECAUSE IT TOOK A WHILE FOR ROSE TO COLLECT THE FIVE OR SIX PINTS OF HER **OWN** BLOOD NEEDED TO CONVINCE US THAT SHE WAS DEAD.

"THEY STORED HER BLOOD IN HER **FREEZER**, SO IT WOULD STILL BE FRESH WHEN THEY NEEDED IT.

"BUT THEY ALWAYS HAD SO MANY PEOPLE OVER, THEY NEEDED **SOME** WAY TO KEEP THEIR GUESTS FROM DISCOVERING THE **BLOOD PACKETS**.

"WHICH IS **WHY** THEY NEEDED TO KEEP HER FREEZER COMPARTMENT LOCKED UP.

"WHICH EXPLAINS WHY I FOUND A **PADLOCK** IN THEIR UTILITY DRAWER THAT FIT THE MATCHING HOLES DRILLED INTO THE FREEZER DOOR!"

THAT *MAY BE* ALL WELL AND GOOD, BUT IT *STILL* DOESN'T GET YOU OFF THE HOOK FOR KEEPING ME IN THE DARK.

I HAD TO, AS LONG AS YOU WERE ONE OF THE *SUSPECTS.*

SUSPECTS? HOW *COULD* I BE? HOW CAN *ANYONE* BE A SUSPECT IN A MURDER THAT NEVER TOOK PLACE?

NOT EVEN *ROSE RED* WOULD FAKE HER OWN DEATH WITHOUT GOOD REASON.

FROM DAY *ONE* OF THE INVESTIGATION I WASN'T LOOKING FOR HER KILLER. I WAS *LOOKING* FOR THE PERSON SHE WAS SO *AFRAID* OF—WHO MADE HER GO TO ALL OF THIS EFFORT.

UNTIL I DETERMINED *THAT,* I COULDN'T RISK TELLING *ANY* OF YOU THAT SHE WAS STILL ALIVE.

SO WHO *WAS* SHE SO AFRAID OF?

ROSE? WANT TO ANSWER *THAT* ONE FOR US?

BLUEBEARD.

WHY HIM?

BECAUSE OF *THIS.*

REMEMBER *THIS,* SNOW? IT'S THE MARRIAGE *CONTRACT* YOUR SISTER SIGNED LAST YEAR, IN RETURN FOR A *CONSIDERABLE* AMOUNT OF MONEY.

HERE, IN A NUTSHELL, IS *WHAT* HAPPENED AND *WHY.*

MOST OF THIS I CAN'T *PROVE,* BUT IT'S ALL BACKED UP BY AT LEAST *SOME* EVIDENCE.

"OVER A YEAR AGO, JACK HAD ANOTHER ONE OF HIS ALL-TOO-NUMEROUS *GET RICH QUICK* SCHEMES. IT WAS AN IDEA FOR ONE OF THOSE DOT-COM STARTUPS, IF YOU CAN *BELIEVE* IT.

"TRUST *JACK* TO TRY TO JUMP ON A *BAND-WAGON* LONG AFTER IT'S PASSED BY."

"STARTUPS LIKE THAT TAKE *MONEY.*"

"AND TYPICALLY JACK TURNS TO HIS *GIRL-FRIEND* TO GET IT."

IT'S A *SURE THING,* HONEY BEAR. AND WHEN *I* GET RICH I CAN PAY *YOU* BACK AND YOU CAN PAY *HIM* BACK.

I DON'T KNOW, JACK...

"IN ORDER TO RAISE THE MONEY JACK NEEDED, ROSE AND JACK *FAKED* A MESSY PUBLIC BREAKUP, AFTER WHICH SHE AGREED TO *MARRY* BLUEBEARD, WHO'D BEEN AFTER HER FOR SOME TIME.

"BUT SHE HAD SOME *CONDITIONS.* SHE WANTED A LOT OF UP-FRONT *DOWRY* MONEY AND THE ENGAGEMENT HAD TO BE KEPT *SECRET* FOR EXACTLY ONE YEAR."

THAT GAVE JACK ENOUGH TIME TO MAKE HIS *FORTUNE*, AND THEN ROSE WOULD PAY BLUEBEARD BACK AND-- RELUCTANTLY-- BREAK OFF THEIR SECRET ENGAGEMENT.

UNFORTUNATELY JACK LOST ALL THAT MONEY, DOWN THE SAME *BLACK HOLE* WHERE EVERYONE ELSE LOST THEIR DOT-COM INVESTMENTS.

SO, AS THE YEAR BEGAN TO RUN OUT-- KNOWING FULL *WELL* THAT A MAN LIKE BLUEBEARD WOULDN'T SIMPLY *FORGIVE* THE DEBT, OR THE *UNETHICAL* WAY THEY EXTRACTED THE MONEY FROM HIM-- JACK AND ROSE COOKED UP THEIR SCHEME TO GET HER OUT OF HER IMPENDING *NUPTIALS*.

FAKING YOUR *DEATH?* ARE YOU FUCKING *KIDDING* ME, ROSE?

HOW LONG DID YOU IMAGINE *THAT* WOULD WORK?

WE NEEDED A WAY TO BUY MORE *TIME*-- JUST UNTIL WE FIGURED OUT ANOTHER WAY TO...

TO LAND YOURSELF IN *MUCH* MORE TROUBLE THAN YOU WERE IN *ORIGINALLY?*

NEITHER ROSE NOR JACK EARNED RENOWN FOR THEIR *INTELLIGENCE*. WORKING TOGETHER, THEY COULDN'T *HELP* BUT REACH NEW LOWS OF IMBECILITY.

OH YEAH, PEASANT SCUM? IF *I'M* SO DUMB AND *YOU'RE* SO SMART, HOW IS IT I *NOW* HAVE THE TITLES AND LANDS *YOU* USED TO *OWN?*

WHY DO YOU THINK THEY CALL IT DUMB *LUCK*, PRINCE KNUCKLE-DRAGGER?

ENOUGH OF THIS! *STOP* IT, BOTH OF YOU! *ALL* OF YOU!

BY GOD I'LL HAVE ORDER **NOW**, OR I'LL HAVE SOME HEADS ON THE **CHOPPING** BLOCK!

MISTER WOLF, IS THERE ANYTHING **ELSE** YOU'VE YET TO REVEAL?

NO, I'VE PRETTY MUCH TOLD **ALL** OF IT.

THEN WHAT ARE WE TO DO **NOW**?

WHO KNOWS? I'VE DONE **MY** JOB BY FIGURING EVERYTHING OUT. IT'S UP TO **YOU** AND **SNOW** TO WORK OUT WHAT TO **DO** ABOUT IT.

BUT I HAVE SOME **SUGGESTIONS**, IF YOU'D CARE TO HEAR ABOUT THEM -- IN **PRIVATE**.

I'M THE INJURED PARTY HERE. I'VE BEEN CHEATED OUT OF MY MONEY **AND** A BRIDE. I'LL HAVE SATISFACTION FROM THESE TWO. **HIS** BLOOD ON MY BLADE, AND **HER** HAND IN MARRIAGE -- AS SHE IS **CONTRACTED** TO DO.

AND **I** HAVE SOME MONEY COMING TOO.

YOU'VE YET TO **PAY** ME THE GLORIOUS **MILLIONS** I'VE EARNED FOR THE RAFFLE OF MY TITLE AND ESTATES.

WE'LL SETTLE ALL OF THAT **LATER**. FOR NOW, IT'S LATE. EVERYONE GO HOME, AND **STAY** THERE.

THE MAYOR, THE SHERIFF AND I WILL MEET TO WORK THINGS OUT -- AND **SUMMON** YOU AS YOU'RE NEEDED -- SO DON'T ANYONE WANDER OFF.

THE NEXT DAY.

ZZZZ

BIGBY, WILL YOU PLEASE QUIT *SNOOPING* AND SIT DOWN?

SORRY, SNOW, BUT I'VE NEVER SEEN YOUR APARTMENT BEFORE.

YOU'VE DONE *WELL* FOR YOURSELF. IT'S NICE. AND *BIG* TOO. MY ENTIRE APARTMENT COULD FIT INSIDE YOUR *BATHROOM*.

I'VE WORKED *HARD* FOR WHAT I'VE EARNED. THIS PLACE IS ONE OF THE FEW *BENEFITS* OF RUNNING THE ENTIRE GODDAMN FABLE COMMUNITY.

NOW *PLEASE* SIT DOWN SO WE CAN FINISH UP.

WHAT'S LEFT TO *DECIDE*? YOU'VE WORKED IT ALL OUT SO THAT *NO ONE* ENDS UP HAPPY.

BUT AT LEAST THE MISERY IS SPREAD *OUT* AS MUCH AS POSSIBLE.

AND KING COLE WILL GO *ALONG* WITH THIS?

THE MAYOR'S JOB IS TO *GLAD-HAND* AND SET GENERAL POLICY. IT'S *MY* JOB TO WORK OUT THE DIRTY *DETAILS*.

HE'LL GO ALONG WITH WHAT I DECIDE.

NO ONE'S GOING TO BE VERY HAPPY WITH YOU AFTER TODAY.

BOO FUCKING HOO. I'LL TRY TO *LIVE* WITH THE LOSS.

WHEN DID *YOU* START CUSSING SO MUCH?

NOW LET'S GET *TO* IT. BRING THEM TO ME IN *THIS* ORDER, AT *THESE* PLACES, AND *I'LL* HANDLE THE ACTUAL *BLOODLETTING*.

DON'T YOU *DARE* LIGHT THAT UNTIL YOU LEAVE.

SO HERE WE ARE, MY *SWEET*, BACK AT THE SAME TABLE, IN THE SAME *PLACE* WHERE WE ORIGINALLY KICKED OFF THE PLAN THAT MADE ME *RICH* AGAIN. *FULL CIRCLE*, YOU MIGHT SAY.

DO YOU *HAVE* MY MONEY?

HERE YOU GO.

I AM THE EGGMAN DINER

DON'T SPEND IT ALL IN ONE PLACE, *DARLING*.

WHERE'S THE *REST*?

THAT'S *ALL* OF IT--LESS THE *PRE-AGREED* FEES AND EX-PENSES OF COURSE.

WHAT SORT OF UNETHICAL *NONSENSE* IS THIS?

THE RAFFLE BROUGHT IN *MILLIONS* AND YET THERE'S *BARELY* THIRTY THOUSAND DOLLARS HERE.

LESS *TWENTY THOUSAND* AND CHANGE. YOU SHOULD HAVE *READ* OUR AGREEMENT MORE *CLOSELY* BEFORE SIGNING IT.

IT ALLOWED ME TO TAKE OUT ALL *REASONABLE* EXPENSES, BEFORE YOU GET YOUR *SHARE*-- AND I AM THE SOLE ARBITRATOR OF WHAT CONSTITUTES A "REASONABLE EXPENSE!"

THE MONEY WE RAISED IS NEEDED TO PAY OFF *BLUEBEARD*, AND THE COST OF THE *INVESTIGATION*. YOU'RE *LUCKY* I GAVE YOU THE LEFTOVERS.

BUT *NONE* OF THAT IS *MY* RESPONSIBILITY!

TOO *BAD*. YOU SHOULD *NEVER* HAVE SLEPT WITH MY SISTER.

NOW, IF I WERE *YOU*, I'D USE WHAT'S *LEFT* TO BUY YOUR TITLE *BACK* FROM JACK. I BET HE CAN BE BOUGHT *CHEAP*, AND YOU'D NEVER MAKE IT AS A *POOR* COMMONER.

BYE, LOVE. YOU'LL PICK UP THE *CHECK*?

THANK YOU, LORD BLUEBEARD, FOR COMING BY SO PROMPTLY.

YOUR *PET WOLF* DIDN'T GIVE ME THE IMPRESSION I HAD ANY *CHOICE* IN THE MATTER.

THIS IS *AMERICA*, WHERE WE *ALL* HAVE FREEDOM OF CHOICE.

FOR *EXAMPLE*, THIS CASE CONTAINS ALL OF THE MONEY YOU ORIGINALLY GAVE TO MY SISTER, AS HER DOWRY-- IN *CASH*.

IF YOU *CHOOSE* TO ACCEPT IT-- AS YOUR *ONLY* REPAYMENT FOR ALL THE WRONGS YOU'VE SUFFERED--THEN EVERYTHING CAN END NICELY.

THERE'S *STILL* THE MATTER OF THE *WEDDING*.

THAT'S *OFF*.

BUT I HAVE A *CONTRACT!*

YES, A CONTRACT YOU *BROKE*.

YOU *PROMISED*, AS ONE OF THE CONDITIONS OF YOUR AGREEMENT WITH MY SISTER, TO KEEP THE ENGAGEMENT A *SECRET*, FOR ONE *YEAR* -- SPECIFICALLY UNTIL THE NIGHT OF THE REMEMBRANCE DAY CELEBRATION.

SO? — SO YOU TOLD BIGBY AND ME ABOUT IT SEVERAL DAYS *BEFORE* THE CELEBRATION.

SNOW WHITE
DIRECTOR OF OPERATIONS

ONLY WHEN WE ALL THOUGHT SHE'D BEEN *MURDERED!* ONLY IN RESPONSE TO YOUR QUESTIONS, IN AN *OFFICIAL* INVESTIGATION!

SO? YOU BROKE THE *CONDITIONS* OF THE CONTRACT, MAKING IT *NULL* AND *VOID.*

YOU'RE LUCKY ENOUGH THAT WE'RE WILLING TO *REIMBURSE* THE MONEY YOU'VE LOST. WE DON'T *HAVE* TO.

I WON'T *STAND* FOR THIS!

THEN I HAVE NO CHOICE BUT TO TAKE *BACK* THE MONEY AND *REINSTATE* THE CHARGES AGAINST YOU, FOR THE *ATTEMPTED MURDER* OF JACK WHILE HE WAS IN *CUSTODY.*

SNOW WHITE
DIRECTOR OF OPERATIONS

UNFORTUNATELY, THAT MEANS YOUR *HEAD* GOES THE WAY OF SO MANY OF YOUR PAST *WIVES'* HEADS.

CHOPPY CHOPPY-- SO *SLOPPY.*

HERE'S THE *DEAL*, KIDS.

YOU *BOTH* GET TO KEEP YOUR HEADS AND STAY OUT OF JAIL.

BUT YOU'RE ON *PROBATION* FOR A YEAR AND YOU EACH OWE *200 HOURS* OF COMMUNITY SERVICE AND *TEN THOUSAND DOLLARS* IN FINES.

WE DON'T *HAVE* THAT KIND OF MONEY.

IT MIGHT AS WELL BE A *MILLION* EACH.

YOU'LL HAVE IT BY THE END OF THE DAY.

MY *SOURCES* TELL ME EX-PRINCE CHARMING IS WILLING TO PAY AT *LEAST* THAT MUCH TO GET HIS LANDS AND TITLE BACK.

SO THAT'S *IT?* NO ONE ENDS UP WITH *ANYTHING?*

YOU END UP WITH YOUR *FREEDOM*, WHICH IS MORE THAN *EITHER* OF YOU DESERVES.

AND YOU KEEP *THAT* MUCH ONLY AS LONG AS YOU *BEHAVE.*

AND WE ALL MANAGED TO LIVE HAPPILY EVER AFTER, AFTER *ALL*-- MORE OR LESS.

LESS RATHER THAN *MORE*, I'M AFRAID.

NO ONE'S *HAPPY*, BUT AT LEAST--MAYBE--WE'VE KEPT THEM FROM *KILLING* EACH OTHER.

THAT'S *GOOD* ENOUGH FOR *ME*.

THIS WAS ONE LONG, EXHAUSTING DAY. I'M OFFICIALLY *BEAT*.

BUT YOU HANDLED YOURSELF *WELL*. AFTER SEEING YOU WORK TODAY, I'M *GLAD* WE'RE ON THE SAME SIDE.

NO, ALL I *DID* WAS THROW MY WEIGHT AROUND. *YOU'RE* THE ONE WHO SAVED THE DAY. YOU FIGURED EVERYTHING *OUT*.

YOU'RE REALLY NOT A HALF-BAD DETECTIVE.

DAMNING ME WITH FAINT *PRAISE?*

SOMETHING LIKE THAT. ONLY--

YES?

THERE'S STILL **ONE** THING I DON'T UNDERSTAND. WHY DID YOU NEED ME TO BE YOUR **DATE** AT THE REMEMBRANCE DAY CELEBRATION?

I **EXPLAINED** THAT AT THE TIME.

NO YOU DIDN'T. YOU SAID IT WAS **NECESSARY** TO HELP YOU SOLVE THE CASE, BUT YOU NEVER EXPLAINED **WHY**. HOW DID THAT **HELP** YOU? WHY WAS IT NECESSARY AT **ALL**?

WELL, I THINK THE REASON SHOULD BE **OBVIOUS**.

THEN I MUST JUST BE A DIM BULB TONIGHT. I NEED THE OBVIOUS **INTERPRETED** FOR ME.

I WANTED YOU TO GO TO THE DAMNED DANCE WITH ME--AS MY DATE.

SERIOUSLY? YOU WERE TOO SHY--OR **AFRAID**--TO ASK ME TO GO TO THE GALA WITH YOU, SO YOU **PRETENDED** IT WAS BUSINESS-RELATED?

YEAH, THAT'S ABOUT IT.

THAT'S **PATHETIC**.

REALLY? I WAS **HOPING** FOR SOMETHING MORE ALONG THE LINES OF, ODDLY, DISARMINGLY **CHARMING**.

WELL IT **WASN'T**. **DON'T** DO IT AGAIN. WE'RE **COLLEAGUES**, AND NOTHING MORE.

FINE.

SERIOUSLY. **NEVER** AGAIN. BACK **OFF**, BIGBY.

OKAY, LADY, I GOT THE MESSAGE. LOUD AND CLEAR.

The End--
FOR NOW.

BY BILL WILLINGHAM

When the invaders flooded into the valley, the old wolf came down from his warm den in the high hills to see what all the fuss was about. It didn't take him long to find the alien soldiers, for they tended to call attention to themselves. They wore suits of dark iron and marched in long, clattering ranks. They burned and pillaged wheresoever they went, enslaving those they could easily capture, while putting all others to the sword — those who resisted, to be sure, but also those who were too lame, too old, or too well educated to make able and subservient workers. The wolf took umbrage at these uncouth intruders, not only because they had the temerity to enter his territory uninvited, but also because they murdered wantonly, without craft or subtlety. In addition they killed or spirited away many of those living in the wooded valley that the wolf had marked in his mind to dine on one day, and such a breach of etiquette could not be endured.

In those days the wolf was still largely ruled by his belly, so he decided to sample a few of the invaders. They were easy enough to bring down, because, for all of his monstrous size, the wolf could strike with great stealth and cunning. In the deep woods between one isolated village and another, he picked off two stragglers as they marched behind a long column, biting easily through their shells of thick plate, and the ring-mail hauberks underneath, like a child crumbles autumn leaves. Once he'd stripped away the outer wrappings, he discovered misshapen, yellow-tusked gobliny things within. They screamed and pleaded and writhed well enough, as he savaged them, and their bones crunched satisfyingly, but their green and warty flesh was foul. Carrion three weeks rotting in the heart of summer tasted better than this!

That night, silent as a shadow, he crept into the army's sprawling encampment, thinking that their more human-looking captains might prove more suitable to his refined palate. He whispered past the watch-fires, ragged troop tents, and posted sentries — both sleeping and alert — until, quite undetected, he reached the camp's innermost ring, where the silken pavilions of the officers could be found. Choosing the biggest tent as the one most likely to house the sweetest confection, he leapt in, without so much as a breath of sound, and surprised a sleeper in his bed. He crunched the man's head first, like a red ripe apple, stifling any possibility of alarm, and then settled in for a long, leisurely repast. But after only a few bites, even this man's flesh proved unsuitable. It was tan and unblemished, but still carried a disturbing taint of corruption. The audacity of these people! Not only do they rob him of his preferred provender, but in turn they fail to provide anything approaching a suitable substitute?

The wolf's rage grew, and long into the night he pondered what to do about it.

In the days that followed, the wolf made himself a determined enemy of the invaders. He ranged far and wide, striking in this place and that, in the dead of night, or under the bright daytime sun. There seemed no pattern to his predations, which only increased the dread sown amongst his new adversaries. Relentlessly he hunted the soldiers and their masters, wherever he could find them — and he found them in abundance, infesting every land and kingdom, no matter how far afield he wandered from his own familiar territory. He slaughtered most of those he caught without hesitation or mercy, but spared a few long enough for questioning. From these he learned little of value. They were the advance forces of a remote and unnamed power — known only to the troops as their emperor — for he was by all accounts a creature bold with ambition and sorcerous might who'd decided to carve for himself a single, grand empire out of all the disparate kingdoms of fable.

"Why do you contend so against us?" one captive pleaded as he struggled helplessly under the wolf's massive forepaws. "For you are the very sort of monster we are commissioned to recruit into our ranks. You could rise high in the empire, commanding legions, or more!"

"Not interested," the wolf growled in return. "Even the highest office in service to another is too low a station for me." And with that the wolf sank his fangs into the captive's

neck. A single, irresistible shake ended the soldier's tremors, instantly transforming living flesh into wet carcass.

Years passed in this fashion. The wolf hunted where he would, and the invaders trembled in their tents. But for all of his rapacious success, the wolf was but a single creature, where the Emperor could field seemingly endless battalions. Lands were methodically conquered and consolidated into the empire, despite his constant harassment. At best he was but an irritant in his unseen adversary's vast game of thrones.

Which isn't to say that his personal campaign went unnoticed in whatever distant country had spawned the invasion. Entire companies of the Emperor's most diabolical soldiers — trolls, giants and worse — were tasked with his capture or destruction. And when he eluded those, fell sorcerers and black-hearted warlocks were dispatched. He led them all a merry chase, and reflected from time to time that his life was good, all things considered.

One day, in the shadow of a range of tall white mountains that looked like the fangs of the Earth, bared to rend the heavens above, the wolf encountered a small force of the Emperor's soldiers escorting a much larger group of captives. They were led in heavy rattling chains, down out of the mountains' girdling foothills, where many tried to escape in recent years. From a concealed spot above the winding trail, the wolf watched them as they passed. The prisoners were wretched and dirty things, dressed in old rags for the most part, and new scars, no doubt received during the rough business of their capture. They stumbled along with bent backs and blank faces, sure signs that they knew, and finally surrendered to, the fate that awaited them — days of torture, to wring from them any information about other fugitives, followed by public execution. It seems the Emperor didn't believe in redemption. Those who resisted the all-too-generous initial welcome into his new regime were never offered a second chance. The guards for their part merely looked bored. They could hardly even be bothered to whip the slowpokes and those who stumbled on the trail's sharp stones. This had become routine duty to them, for many fugitives from many countries converged on this land, believing whispered rumors of a magic avenue of escape hidden somewhere in these rugged

and forbidding hills. They arrived in droves and the soldiers captured them — most of them, anyway — with ease.

From his hiding place the wolf patiently watched and waited as he sniffed the cold pre-winter air for signs of a larger, hidden force. This wouldn't be the first time the enemy had tried to lure him into a trap with such inviting bait as this. He'd grown quite wary over the years. Eventually though, with no sign of other threats in the air, he padded down to the trail and followed the slow procession, silently closing the distance between them.

Nearly midway in the prisoner train, two sisters were chained to the line, one in front of the other. They were both lovely young women — though it was hard to be sure under the dirty clothes and half-dried mud that covered them from head to toe — and resembled each other, except that one had hair as dark as night while the other's was as red as the morning sun. In one other way they differed as well. The dark-haired sister wore a gown of rich velvet and white linen, bespeaking nobility, while the red-haired sister wore a simple peasant dress of rough homespun. Of course, the great leveler of extended hardship and adversity had so reduced each garment to egalitarian rags and tatters that only close and careful examination could determine their disparate origins.

Like the other captives, the sisters marched silently — except for the rattling chains manacled to each wrist and ankle — alone in their thoughts, until a sudden clamor of dying men startled them out of their private reveries. The commotion came from the back of the prisoner train, which abruptly compressed in the center, as those in front stopped to see what occurred in the rear, while those in the rear rushed forward to escape whatever it was back there that was killing the guards and filling the air with such feral, bestial sounds as to chill anyone's soul to the core.

Within the tangled press of panicking captives the dark-haired sister couldn't make out any details of what was happening behind them, other than the occasional glimpse of armored guards rushing from the head of the line towards the screams and clamor at its rear. For the moment she concentrated on holding onto her sister, as they worked together to keep upright, so as not to be trampled underfoot. Then the worst of the sounds died away, leaving only the whimpers of the chained prisoners, and while she was still being jerked and tugged, first one way and then the next, by the chains that attached her to everyone else, the mass of shuddering bodies opened up enough to finally reveal their new danger. A wolf had come amongst them, and such a wolf it was! On all fours it stood as tall as a yearling colt. Its fur was black, shading to brownish-gray on its flanks and belly, but at the moment most of its front end was painted red with the blood of the dozen guardsmen who'd so ruthlessly ruled their lives for many days past — right up until a moment ago. To a man they were all dead — savagely dismembered — their parts scattered up and down the trail, and the beast that destroyed them now stood no more than a pace or two from the center of the line, and the two sisters caught there. The women were held in place, stretched out to the limits of their shackles, as their chained companions on each end of the line tried to rush away from the middle, in an attempt to escape the terrible thing that stood amongst them. Some tried to run or crawl away, in both directions on the trail, while others tried to claw their way up the steep embankment on its hillward side. Still others simply surrendered to their certain doom and dropped where they were, trying to curl up or cover themselves as best they could. But the sisters didn't attempt to run or crawl or in any other way try to escape. Perhaps they knew that such attempts would be futile, or they found reserves of courage, or perhaps they simply knew something of what the cornered deer knows after the long chase, when it has finally resigned itself to becoming food for the lion. Whatever the reason, they stood where they were and stared into the yellow eyes that seemed to impale them in place. Entranced, they watched the steaming vapor of recent murder rise from each side of its red-wet muzzle. They listened to each ragged breath that issued from the bellows of its massive chest.

Then a sudden loss of tension in the chains seemed to break the dark one out of her spell — if only for a moment — but that was long enough for her to reach down by her feet where one of the guard's swords had landed during the carnage. She deftly snatched up the curved blade, slippery with its former owner's blood.

"Stay back, dire beast!" the dark sister cried. "My husband taught me well how to use this!" She held it in both hands, boldly brandishing it towards the wolf.

"I don't believe you," the wolf replied, and was that a tone of humor that colored its deep voice? It didn't attack her, but neither did it back away, or in any way seem concerned about the threatening blade held in a young woman's trembling hands.

"You will if you come closer and I chop you down."

"You misunderstand," the wolf replied, the grin of his long muzzle revealing rows of sharp fangs — the largest longer than a grown man's fingers. "I don't believe you've a husband. Though you're clearly no maiden, I can tell with a whiff and a sniff that it's been long years since you've visited anyone's marriage bed."

"My *former* husband!" the woman said. Under the caked grime, twin apples of ripening anger colored her alabaster cheeks.

"Put down your sword, woman. I doubt you could hurt me with it. But if you'll hold out your arms, I'll bite those shackles off you. Quit trembling so! I'm not going to eat you, or these other mewling creatures. It amuses me much more these days to frustrate the Emperor and his legions by spiriting his desired conquests safely out from his clutches. You two aren't from this land — your accents mark you as distant strangers — and yet here you are. I'll bet you've come hoping to find a certain witch's cave of legend. One with many twisting passages that lead to many distant worlds — at least one of which is far beyond the Emperor's reach and possibly even his knowledge."

"I'm amazed that you would know of such a place." This time it was the red-haired woman who spoke. Imitating her sister she had taken advantage of the moment to look for weapons within reach, but no other such device had fallen close enough.

The wolf ignored their efforts at self-defense, but suddenly dashed to nip at those on either end, still stretching out the chains in their efforts to escape. Eventually he herded them back into a loose and fearful cluster that for the most part left the long central chain hanging limp between each captive. Finally, when this was done, he returned to his former place, sat where he had been standing, and answered the red-haired sister.

"I not only know of it, I'm the only one who can still find it, for the witch that made it is long gone, having passed through it to safety many years ago. And because she wanted none of the Emperor's minions following after, she left it cloaked in myriad spells and glamours that cause anyone seeking it to become misdirected and turned around so thoroughly as to be completely frustrated. But I can go there, straight and true, because I secretly followed the old hag that long lost day and marked the trail as only a wolf can."

"Then you are the one that we heard of — the great and terrible guardian of the way," the dark sister said. She hadn't lowered the point of her borrowed blade.

"You look like you expected someone else."

"We'd heard that you were a giant."

"I'm hardly tiny."

"And that you had at least three heads," the red-haired one said, "and by merely looking at you directly, we would be turned to stone."

"Stories do grow in the telling."

"And is the legend also false that you charge a dear price from those you allow to pass on to safety — to the unreachable world?" the dark one said.

"Not entirely, but it's not a matter of payment so much as precaution. The Emperor and his sorcerers have many devious ways to disguise his agents. He's often tried to slip one by me, and there's only one sure way to tell if you're genuine refugees, or more of his creatures in sheep's clothing."

"And what would that be?"

"I'll need a taste — just a little nip from each of you. No matter what shape they began in, or what form in which they present themselves, all of his minions have an unmistakable taint to their flesh. Since you two are so fair, under the accumulated dirt and grime of your recent trials, you'll want to pick a spot where the scar won't show."

"How are we to know that we can trust you, dread wolf?"

"I have no idea, but you'd better decide soon, or any number of bad things could happen. More soldiers could arrive, too numerous for me to overcome, I could grow bored and decide to leave all of you here, to your own devices — or I could grow hungry again and decide to stay."

For the first time since picking it up, the dark woman let the point of her blade drop, perhaps just an inch or two, as her look of fear and determination slowly, reluctantly gave way to something else.

———◆———

Two long centuries later the wolf was prowling the deep dark woods of his new home, in a wild land called Carpathia, when a quiet rustling of underbrush alerted him to the approach of two people. Even from downwind their scents reached him long before they did, identifying one as a stranger and one who seemed distantly familiar.

"You might as well finish coming forward," the wolf grumbled. "You've no chance of outrunning me now, should I decide to eat you, no matter what your starting distance."

The underbrush parted enough to admit two people into the small glade in which the wolf paused, under the spreading canopy of a great oak — a giant of lost ages that painted everything below in deep shadow. The first of the wolf's visitors was an achingly beautiful woman, with skin of whitest porcelain and silken hair darker than a raven's secret heart. She wore an expensive gown of charcoal gray, embroidered in dancing loops and swirls of burgundy thread. It was bowed out by any number of petticoats beneath — a ridiculous contrivance, the wolf thought, in which to go tramping through the woods. Over the dress she wore a long traveling cape, lined in white silk.

Her companion was dressed in similar opulence. He was a tall, slender, aristocratic fellow in matching breeches and waistcoat of powder blue, decorated with enough golden buttons, at the breast, waist and cuffs, to sate the avarice of ancient Midas himself. His vest was also of gold cloth and sported twin rows of even more gold buttons. He wore a broad-brimmed cap, set just so at a jaunty angle. It was of midnight blue, trimmed in more gold, and there was a long feather stuck through its band. He carried a long clay pipe and smoked it furiously, puffing an endless fog of white smoke into the air, almost obscuring his too-handsome features.

"Once long ago you promised not to eat me, Gaffer Wolf," the woman said, through a shy and tentative smile. In that instant the wolf recognized her.

"Only because sparing you then served a higher purpose," the wolf said. "But I no longer spend my days confounding the wishes of that hidden adversary in his far-off empire. I've returned to my former ways, and you're no longer guaranteed safe passage."

Leaving his pipe firmly clamped between his white and perfect teeth, the gentleman's hands drifted down to hover around two bulges distorting his waistcoat that the wolf hadn't noticed at first glance.

"Do you imagine you can retrieve whatever weapons you've concealed there before I can close my jaws around your throat?" the wolf said.

"I doubt you'll find my neck to your taste," the gentleman replied, showing not a hint of fear, "but try it if you must. It won't do me any permanent harm, and you'll be too close to avoid the twin shots of lead I've prepared for you."

"Stop such talk this instant," the woman said. "We didn't travel all this way for anyone to end up shot or eaten."

"Nature will win out," the wolf growled.

"Perhaps so, unless one has a way to change your nature," the woman said. "In any case I'm glad you finally decided to come over to this world."

"I had to. The Emperor's pet warlocks refined their methods of locating me over the years, until it finally became too dangerous even for me to remain there, prowling the numberless lands that had fallen under his heel. And since by that time there were rumors that other passageways to this world had been discovered, I decided my duty was done and it was time to see what sort of place I'd been sending folks to."

"And yet you chose to remain alone, in such a remote land as this?" the woman said. "We had the devil's own time finding you."

The wolf noted that the man moved each time he did, always shifting so as to keep positioned close enough to quickly interpose himself between wolf and woman. The fellow was a puzzle. For the first time in his memory he couldn't decipher a potential opponent's mood and intentions by the scent he gave off. There was a gentleman's cologne of course, but that couldn't mask his natural telltale musks — or at least it couldn't in any past encounter with such men. But beneath this man's sickly sweet perfume the wolf detected nothing — no fear at all, which was surprising

enough, but nothing else either. He turned to the woman again, whom he could still read easily.

"I purposely chose a home far away from those I'd sent here," he said, "so as not to let my hunger undo all of the work I'd done to save them. Here I'm free to hunt the mundane people of this land. They're a superstitious folk that blame everything I do on some fanciful local count who's rumored to be some fell spirit returned from the dead. It means I'm left alone for the most part, and he actually enjoys the notoriety. We visit from time to time. He's not a bad fellow and a good conversationalist, for when I want news of the wider world."

He faced the woman, but all of his attention was focused on her strange companion. He'd seen what these new things — these guns could do. He had no doubt they could do him great harm. If violence was required, he decided he'd first spring at the fellow's waist, rather than his neck. If he could crunch the pistols first, then he'd likely have the two of them in his power — no matter what his strange nature.

"You saved so many of us over the years — the centuries, in fact," the woman said. "I don't believe anyone who could do so much good can be such a monster as you present yourself to be. You belong among us, Gaffer Wolf, among those you saved and other refugees from the lost lands. That's why we've come here, to invite you to take your rightful place back among your own kind. We've started something in the far colonies — the New World. We've formed a community of Fables — two communities, actually — separated by distance, but as one in spirit and purpose. Those of us who can pass as normal humans live together in a remote town called New Amsterdam, far away from the hustle and bustle of this world. Those of us who can't pass as human live in a secret colony deep in the wilderness, in a place so remote that civilization will never overtake it."

"So you long for my company, woman, but plan to send me off to live amongst the animals, far away from you?"

"Not at all," she said and began to blush with embarrassment. "There have been dissenting opinions, threatening to destroy our community, before it begins. In point of fact the experiment is about to fall apart over the matter of what to do with you. On one hand you saved so many of us. On the other hand, your predations in the homelands were truly monstrous, and it's for those crimes that the wilderness colony won't have you. Of all the fell creatures who've escaped to this world, they fear you the most. But what we're attempting is predicated on the notions of equality for all, beginning with a universal pardon of all past crimes, debts and grievances. If one of us is singled out as not worthy of amnesty, then we're back where we started: picking and choosing and counting up past crimes. The community is still fragile and will surely crumble because of this division amongst us, perhaps not this year or the next, but inevitably. Since one colony won't have you, the other one must — but you'll have to be able to pass as human."

"And there's the rub," the wolf said.

"It can be done," the woman said. "You can live as a human, if you choose to." From under her cape she withdrew an ancient iron knife. Its blade was pitted and scarred and looked ready to crumble away in the next breeze. The wolf stiffened when he spied it, reflexively gathering himself to spring — either at her or at the man (or away as fast as he could run) he didn't know yet.

"What's the purpose of that?" he said.

"You found it necessary to bite me once long ago," she said, "so now it's my turn to bite back. This blade is tainted with an ancient magic — an enchantment that lets men walk as wolves."

"I've encountered those impostors, once or twice. They didn't impress me."

"The witch who sold this to me — at a very dear price I might add — said the curse... uhm, the enchantment should work as well in the other direction. A wolf can walk as a man."

"Why should I ever want to do that?"

"That's what we're here to discuss," she said. "And we're prepared to stay long enough to resolve it one way or another. Our hired coach is parked on the roadway down below. Can you direct us to nearby lodgings?"

"Perhaps his friend the count will volunteer shelter to a pair of noble cousins from distant lands," the gentleman said.

The wolf was still getting used to all of the manifest irritations of his new shape when they made the sea crossing. He continuously tugged at and scratched under his woolen frock coat when he'd take his turns on deck. The woman — who turned out to be named after a type of weather in which hunting was typically bad — seldom left her cabin. She didn't like sea travel and claimed the constant pitching and rolling worked ills on her stomach. The wolf discovered he rather enjoyed it. He often encountered the strange gentleman on deck, who seemed not to be bothered by anything, as long as he could keep his ever-present pipe lit. He claimed to have too many names and titles to bother the wolf with and invited him to use Feathertop, which is how he was known amongst most of the Fables. The wolf never felt entirely at ease in the man's company, which Feathertop also noticed and remarked upon one day on the pitching deck.

"I was chosen to accompany the princess on this journey because, of all of the Fables living in this world, I'd be the one most safe from you, if you truly turned out to be monstrous again. I'm not really made of the sorts of things you like to eat." He wouldn't expand on those cryptic comments.

"But as long as we're trading personal secrets," he went on to say, "why don't you tell me why you really chose to come back with us? Though I fancy myself no mean rhetorician, I don't believe either her ladyship or myself argued you into doing anything you hadn't already set your mind to do. The truth now. Why are you here?"

The wolf didn't answer. Instead he turned his face into the gusting rain of a summer squall that had overtaken them, and he thought again about the tiny wisp of a girl, cloaked in equal parts caked grime and foolish bravado, on that long-ago mountain trail, prepared to fight off a ravening monster with but a thin sliver of borrowed steel. And he wondered why, of all the people he'd encountered in his long life, he couldn't quite get her scent out of his mind, no matter the passing of years. He stayed late on deck that night as the tiny wooden ship rode bravely over the rolling swells towards the New World.